Inclusive Design for Historic Buildings

Architectural Approaches
to Accessibility

Inclusive Design for Historic Buildings

Architectural Approaches to Accessibility

David Bonnett and Pauline Nee

THE CROWOOD PRESS

First published in 2021 by
The Crowood Press Ltd
Ramsbury, Marlborough
Wiltshire SN8 2HR

enquiries@crowood.com
www.crowood.com

British Library Cataloguing-in-Publication Data
A catalogue record for this book is available from the British Library.

ISBN 978 1 78500 900 6

Cover design: Maggie Mellett

Typeset by Simon and Sons
Printed and bound in India by Replika Press Pvt. Ltd.

Contents

The Queen's House

THE WIDE RANGE AND CLEAR PRESENTATION of well-designed projects in this book will make it an invaluable resource for architects and students, but I hope it will be equally inspiring and informative to those who are responsible for historic buildings, for whom accessibility should be an essential priority.

The examples provide ample evidence of what can be achieved and their success should encourage those who take on the challenge of making historic buildings more inclusive. Collectively, they establish a standard for future projects that is a matter of social justice when we consider the opportunities in life that are denied when access is difficult or impossible.

Drawing on their long experience and using a case study approach, David Bonnett and Pauline Nee demonstrate conclusively that inclusive design can be both elegant and effective. They set out clearly the key elements of inclusive design, establishing the context and providing a checklist for practising architects that is designed to ensure that all necessary considerations are addressed.

Their brief history of legislation describes the successes and failures of campaigns to put access on the national agenda over the last fifty years, recognizing the important contribution of organizations like Historic England. The book also makes apparent the role that policy-makers – and the agencies and funders like the National Lottery Heritage Fund that help transform policy into practice – have played. I'm particularly proud of the contribution of Arts Council England over a long period, noting that so many of the case study projects have benefited from Arts Council and National Lottery funding.

Our role in supporting inclusivity in capital projects goes beyond the provision of financial resource. Encouraging ambition and creativity in cultural organizations that are working towards access is integral to our approach. For many of the case studies in this book, and other capital projects supported by Arts Council England, the key to achieving inclusive design has been a commitment to partnership working – learning from people with disabilities in their communities about what access and inclusion means to them.

As this book makes clear, effective consultation is fundamental to good design. The systematic consultation method, which was devised by the Arts Council and is highlighted here, should generate inclusive solutions for improving historic buildings.

I urge all those interested in our historic legacy to consult this book. I believe it will inspire those involved in the design process to approach accessibility challenges with confidence. It should also encourage custodians of historic buildings to prepare demanding briefs that will lead to high-quality design in buildings that welcome all and embrace the social model of disability.

Nicholas Serota, Chair, Arts Council England

OPPOSITE: Visitors moving towards the new accessible entrance at Queens House Greenwich, located below the famous Horseshoe steps. (Illustration: John Darvill, RIBA MSAI)

IN AUTUMN 2004 THE CENTRE FOR ACCESSIBLE Environments (CAE) published the 100th issue of its quarterly journal, *Access by Design*. The editorial opening by CEO Sarah Langton-Lockton modestly set out, perhaps for the first time, a definition of inclusive design to 'shed light on this simple but for many, still an elusive concept'. There were five principles, the last of which says, 'Inclusive design aims to provide buildings and environments that are safe, convenient, equitable and enjoyable to use by everyone, regardless of ability, age or gender'.

Significantly, that same year the Royal Institute of British Architects (RIBA) adopted the principles by setting up the RIBA Inclusive Design Award. Two years later in 2006, the Commission for Architecture and the Built Environment (CABE) expanded on the concept yet further, concluding that inclusive design 'creates new opportunities to deploy creative and problem-solving skills'. This last point exactly captures what this book is about. It is written for architects, surveyors and others involved in creatively solving the problems presented by historic buildings that prevent them from being accessible to everyone.

The book will be of interest to students and practitioners alike. In the early chapters it makes the point that the UK's substantial number of historic listed buildings are still in use as places of work, education, entertainment, worship and more and that in order to retain and enhance their value to society they must function inclusively. How this challenging ambition can be reconciled with the long-standing objectives of building conservation is explained.

To better understand the concept of inclusive design, the book sets out the elements that need to be met by any building – old or new – for it to be inclusive. This is, in effect, a way of testing a design that can be applied at the outset of a project, a process usually referred to as an access audit. How this process is undertaken is explained, on-site for an existing building, but equally well on-plan for a new building.

The main section of the book relies on twenty-six listed building case studies, most of which have involved the author over the last twenty-five years. Each study is focused primarily on achieving step-free access into the historic building where originally there was none. Other case studies look at internal circulation. This book focuses on step-free access, as the changes necessary to achieve this are more likely to have an impact on the historic fabric. Of course, for a building to be truly accessible, the designer must also address the needs of those with sensory, ambulatory or intellectual disabilities. Such considerations are described briefly in some of the case studies but are addressed more fully in other publications.

Despite the considerable differences between each building and the solutions devised, a pattern can be discerned. The skills applied by the various project architects and the solutions arrived at all appear to be different, but they are not. By analysis the book identifies five typologies that recur. This method of

OPPOSITE: The Royal Festival Hall on London's South Bank.

analysis will be of particular interest to those applying their problem-solving skills for the first time as students of architecture, but also for creative people in practice. The case studies demonstrate how ideas have successfully been brought to fruition, achieving step-free accessibility to help ensure continued use of the building, while at the same time respecting the historic building fabric. Many of the projects have received awards and provide excellent reference for projects yet to come.

The final part of the book looks at consultation, a process well understood by architects in relation to their clients, but less well understood, if at all, in relation to building users, least of all disabled users. The relatively recent history and social context of how this kind of user consultation gained credibility is described, and in particular how it can so helpfully be applied to historic buildings projects to better understand priorities for change.

The book concludes by examining the social dynamics that first brought the concept of inclusive design into being, sufficiently so for it to become the subject of legislation and regulations, how these might change in the future, and what new concepts might emerge. The authors are both members of David Bonnett Associates, an architectural practice dedicated to inclusive design. They hope that this book might stimulate yet wider interest and understanding of the subject, one that has kept the practice happily busy since 1995 when the Disability Discrimination Act first came into force. Now, twenty-five years on, that legislation continues to have an impact on our buildings, how they are designed and how they can best serve society. At the time of writing, the Covid-19 pandemic will oblige us to ask yet more from our historic buildings and think afresh about the contribution they might make.

OUR SINCERE THANKS GO TO THE FOLLOW-ing without whom writing this book would have been impossible:

Struan Cameron for his invaluable support in all things to do with graphic design, image research and organization of material; colleagues at DBA for their contribution to some of the projects, most notably the late Stuart Schlindwein-Robinson but also Rachael Marshall, John Darvill and Helen Allan; David's wife Susan: for her unfailing support and encouragement and some of the photographs; finally to the many wonderful and demanding clients, architects and project managers who, between them, have achieved such significant changes over the last twenty-five years.

Chapter One

Conservation and Legislation

Background

Legislation to protect the UK's historic buildings was first introduced in 1882. Although it took another century before legislation was enacted that would provide easier access for disabled visitors to these buildings, inclusive design is now a fundamental consideration whenever an historic building is being adapted, upgraded or remodelled.

The reasons for this change in attitude are varied: as disability campaigners became more vociferous in the 1970s and 1980s, public opinion shifted and started to regard access as a human right and a social expectation. Legislation followed the public mood, most importantly with the introduction of the Disability Discrimination Act in 1995 and the Equality Act in 2010. The 1990 Planning Act provided the green light for planning authorities to include access as a requirement in their development plans. Meanwhile, a requirement for access was introduced to the building regulations in 1985, albeit originally limited to new buildings and extensions to existing buildings.

There are over 500,000 listed buildings in England alone. Although a proportion of these will be uninhabited or function solely as tourist attractions, many are providing a similar function to that provided when first constructed, whether as a government office, a university, a place of worship, theatre, museum or train station. Politicians, office workers, students, theatregoers and passengers now expect to have full access to their place of work, study, entertainment or travel.

Financial considerations, unsurprisingly, have played a significant role in the creation of accessible environments. Building owners and managers may adopt the concept in order to minimize the risk – and potential cost – of being refused planning permission or building control approval. In other instances they will be keen to attract financial support from grant-awarding organizations. The Arts Council and the Heritage Lottery Fund (HLF), among others, have made access a condition of their grant awards, resulting in the flourishing of high quality, inclusive design.

These financial considerations have been augmented by the growing significance of the 'grey pound' in sustaining ticket sales in historic venues throughout the country. The importance of historic buildings to both civic pride and to the UK economy leads to significant investment. One clear example of this is London's West End, which has the highest concentration of theatres anywhere in the world; the majority are Victorian or Edwardian. The theatre district contributes around £1 billion to the UK economy. For tourism to flourish it is essential that no visitor to such venues be unnecessarily excluded. It is to be hoped that the 2020 pandemic does not have a long-term negative impact on the UK tourist industry.

The UK is deservedly proud of its international reputation for good access – as highlighted during the 2012 Olympic and Paralympic Games. There is still a long way to go but the relative ease with which a visitor – whether in a wheelchair, using crutches, accompanied by a guide dog or with any other physical, sensory or intellectual disability – can now gain access to a large proportion of our historic buildings is testament to the determination and energy of various groups. The disability lobby, combined with the response of politicians, the resolve of funders, the open mindedness of the heritage lobby and the creativity of building professionals, have all contributed to the improving position.

OPPOSITE: Sir John Soane's Museum by Lincoln's Inn Fields. (Photo: Tony Hisgett from Birmingham, UK, CC BY 2.0, via Wikimedia Commons)

The Role of Designers

The passing of the Disability Discrimination Act in 1995 required that the needs of all users should be considered from the outset. It was recognized that buildings must be designed and adapted in order to meet legal requirements and social expectations while achieving the highest standards of design. This aspiration for a creative response to access was expressed in 2006 by CABE.

> Inclusive Design is about making places everyone can use. The way places are designed affects our ability to move, see, hear and communicate effectively. Inclusive Design aims to remove the barriers that create undue effort and separation. It enables everyone to participate equally, confidently and independently in everyday activities. An inclusive approach to design offers new insights into the way we interact with the built environment. It creates new opportunities to deploy creative and problem-solving skills.
>
> *CABE, 2006*

Disability
Discrimination Act
1995

CHAPTER 50

First Published 1995
Reprinted 2002

The Disability Discrimination Act 1995 required building owners by law to ensure that where their buildings provided a service it should be accessible.

Each of the projects described in this book demonstrates that good accessibility requires a team approach, involving heritage specialists, building designers, operational managers and users. In many instances the way a building is managed will have the greatest influence on its accessibility. By embracing full access, providing clear information on the website, training staff, ensuring that specialist equipment is regularly serviced, and listening to feedback, all users – whether disabled or not – will benefit and hopefully appreciate their engagement with the historic environment.

The Response to Legislation and Regulation

The response of the statutory sector to the increased demand for access has generally been constructive, with the national heritage bodies, CADW, Historic Scotland and Historic England, together with a number of local authorities, producing guidance and providing training, as well as engaging creatively, on the whole, with campaigners, designers and others in exploring options for ensuring full access.

While design solutions have been wide-ranging – and we have probably all been disappointed by the insertion of a poorly designed ramp or a badly positioned platform lift – the professions have, on the whole, taken up the CABE gauntlet to deploy their creative and problem-solving skills in providing sensitive insertions or complementary additions to our best loved buildings.

Building owners and managers who may have baulked at the anticipated expense (frequently negligible) or the potential statutory objections (generally minimal) often become enthusiastic patrons of inclusive design. It is unknown whether this is because they are happy to see more diverse usage, whether it reduces the cost and aggravation of making specialist provision or whether it results in greater ticket sales, increased attendance at church or more satisfied employees.

The Houses of Parliament are a popular attraction for visitors, but are also working buildings with offices, the chambers and all supporting facilities.

Uniting Protection and Access: A Brief Introduction to Heritage Protection

The UK has long celebrated its wealth of historic structures. The Society of Antiquaries was set up as early as 1707, its aim, as set out in its 1751 Royal Charter, to foster 'the encouragement, advancement and furtherance of the study and knowledge of the antiquities and history of this and other countries'.

In 1877 William Morris, with others, held the inaugural meeting of the Society for the Protection of Ancient Buildings (SPAB) and expressed concern that well-meaning architects were scraping away the historic fabric of too many buildings in their zealous 'restorations'. SPAB continues to be a significant voice in the world of conservation, its philosophy of conservative repair and minimal intervention having a strong impact on heritage thinking. Five years after the creation of SPAB, the 1882 Ancient Monuments Act gave protection to twenty-one monuments and in 1895 the Royal Commission on Historic Monuments commenced its inventory of pre-1707 buildings.

In the early twentieth century, following the creation of the National Trust and other conservation societies, legislation was extended, often as a result of local campaigns. In 1947 the Town and Country Planning Act responded to the growing calls for adequate protection, instituting a statutory list of significant buildings and introducing the requirement for Listed Building Consent.

In 1983 the National Heritage Act created English Heritage (now Historic England) to protect and promote the historic environment: its equivalents in Scotland and Wales are Historic Scotland and CADW. The 2012 National Planning Policy Framework, updated in 2019, requires that planning authorities should recognize that heritage assets are an irreplaceable resource and conserve them in a manner appropriate to their significance.

Improving Access for All in Buildings of Historic Significance

It is against this background of statutory protection, combined with academic study and effective public campaigns to safeguard the nation's historic legacy, that legislation to improve access for all was introduced toward the end of the twentieth century.

Despite the philosophy of minimal intervention in historic buildings, the demand for accessibility was accepted, and even welcomed, by heritage professionals. Many responded positively, providing both guidance and training. Details of key publications, produced by heritage specialists and others, are listed in the Bibliography.

The 2010 Equality Act, which replaced the 1995 Disability Discrimination Act, provides protection from discrimination in the accessing of services in education and in employment. Those who have duties under the Act may need to adapt their premises to ensure that they do not discriminate. The Equalities Act does not specify design standards. However, service providers and employers may need to consider wider equality obligations when undertaking design work.

The requirement for accessibility does not override the need to obtain statutory approvals, such as Listed Building Consent, Conservation Area Consent or Scheduled Monument Consent. The importance of the historic fabric is summarized in the Building Regulations, Approved Document M, Access to and Use of Buildings, first introduced in 1985:

> The need to conserve the special characteristics of … historic buildings must be recognised. They are a finite resource with cultural importance. In such work the aim should be to improve accessibility where and to the extent that it is practically possible, always provided that the work does not prejudice the character of the historic building, or increase the risk of long-term deterioration to the building fabric or fittings.

Approved Document M, Volume g2 Para 0.18

While full access is a necessary ambition, full compliance with access recommendations for some nationally important buildings may not be possible, or even desired. Where this is the case, it may be preferable to investigate options for mitigating access difficulties by providing high quality and creative visitor information, or exploring managed support.

Such an approach is very much the exception. This book will examine a variety of high profile buildings and their settings, many of them Grade 1 listed. Without exception, these demonstrate effective and welcome solutions to improved access. Acting responsibly, the architects and access consultants – as well as the clients, funding bodies and statutory authorities – were committed to retaining and enhancing the special interest of the building in question. It was recognized that when alterations were deemed necessary or desirable they should emanate from a thorough understanding of the historic and architectural significance of the facility in question. When such an approach is combined with an understanding of the needs of all users – and note that very few historic buildings have not been altered by the introduction of electricity or running water – these alterations demonstrate that it is possible to achieve elegant, effective and frequently understated solutions that benefit all.

An innovative approach can be of particular value when working with historic buildings. The most successful solutions are frequently the result of heritage advisors engaging creatively with access groups, designers and others in exploring options for ensuring full access. Such collaboration will ensure that our important historic buildings have a viable future, enabling them to function as working buildings as well as tourist attractions.

The approach to assessing the accessibility of an existing building is similar to the approach of conservation specialists who categorize the historic significance of each element of the building. It is not uncommon for intrusive elements that detract from the overall significance of a building to provide opportunities for the inclusion of access improvements.

As outlined in the introduction, the most creative solutions will fall short of expectations if the resultant building is not well managed. For instance, in an internationally renowned museum the beautifully designed accessible WC has a notice on its door advising would-be users to find an attendant to open it up. At a seminar on platform lifts, arranged for the benefit of Oxford colleges, facilities managers bemoaned not only the low cost and unattractive lifts that are frequently specified but also the maintenance contracts that employ lift engineers unfamiliar with non-standard lift mechanisms.

Access to a building commences when someone decides to visit and enquires about access provision, maybe by looking at the website or phoning for advice. A clear website, with advice on accessible transport options and car parking, as well as guidance on any barriers that may be encountered, is essential. Equally, it is vital to have well-trained staff, who can advise on special provision, ranging from the location of wheelchair seating in a theatre to the supply of vibrating pillows in a hotel to alert the hard of hearing in case of fire.

The International Position

Heritage protection is guided by international charters developed throughout the twentieth century, largely under the umbrella of International Council on Monuments and Sites (ICOMOS), an international organization created to develop best practice in the conservation and management of cultural sites. One of the most significant of these is the Burra Charter first adopted by Australia ICOMOS in 1979 and most recently updated in 2013.

While there is no similar international body guiding inclusive design, many countries have adopted legislation that is broadly similar in tone

ICOMOS
international council on monuments and sites

ICOMOS is an international organization created to develop best practice in the conservation and management of cultural sites.

and ambition to UK legislation. From the 1960s to the 1980s, the US was probably the country with the most effective culture of access, developed as part of the Civil Rights movement and in response to the disabilities arising from two World Wars followed by the polio outbreaks of the 1940s and the war in Vietnam. To encapsulate their determination to make access provision mainstream, US campaigners coined the phrase 'universal design', an aspiration to create an environment to benefit all.

In 1990 the US passed the Americans with Disabilities Act. The UK's Disability Discrimination Act followed this in 1995. Since 2000 the European Commission Directive against discrimination sets a minimum standard that applies across the European Union. National laws determine the exact form of implementation. The EU Directive, paralleling the UK Disability Discrimination Act, requires employers (and training providers) to provide 'reasonable accommodations' to meet the needs of disabled people.

Recent consultation with campaigners in the US suggests that the UK has overtaken the US in its commitment to universal design, particularly when it comes to historic buildings. It is not clear why this is so, perhaps because the US has fewer historic buildings of note and is therefore more 'protective' of them; perhaps the influence of public funding organizations, such as the HLF, is lacking in the US, where most building work is privately funded.

The approach in other countries varies. Best practice in terms of access is encouraged, often even required by law but often unsupported by expectation and ambition. It will be interesting, and hopefully heartening, to see how this approach develops in the twenty-first century.

Historic Buildings in Everyday Use

THE NUMBER OF HISTORIC BUILDINGS IN THE UK is considerable, with many of them – half a million at least – protected to some extent from change by their Listed status. Furthermore many of these buildings continue in use as first intended; as places of worship, of course, but also as offices, learning institutes, theatres, museums and even as railway stations. But they all serve the public and in this they all share a common responsibility to meet the standards currently expected of public buildings – accessibility included – regardless of whether or not they are listed. Herein lies the challenge that requires a combination of creative thinking, problem-solving skills and sound judgement based on experience.

This book hopes to demonstrate that in most instances it is possible to meet the seemingly opposing demands of heritage protection and accessibility. It will be clear that a creative and often innovative approach may lead to successful solutions and ensure that the majority of historic buildings have a viable future, enabling them to welcome a wider range of users. We want to celebrate our historic buildings but we do not want to preserve them in aspic. In the past we happily added electrics, central heating and toilets. Today, we may take more care of the historic fabric when we make the changes necessary

to ensure accessibility but we cannot ignore our obligations to every user, able-bodied or not.

It is a premise of inclusive design that it achieves its purpose unobtrusively. It is to be hoped that most visitors to a venue do not realize that the ease with which they entered the building, bought tickets and then enjoyed the exhibition or performance and café or bar was due, in large part, to the fact that the venue was designed to meet the needs of all who enter, not just the able-bodied.

This chapter examines a range of building types, highlighting why change is necessary and pointing to a range of buildings where change, whether minor modification or major transformation, has ensured that the building remains suitable for use in the twenty-first century.

Government Buildings

Government buildings may range from offices, with or without public access, to civic buildings of international repute. Unsurprisingly, many government institutions are located in buildings of historic importance. Both central and local government are aware that they need

Access improvements have been made to the Palace of Westminster over the years. Now, as part of a comprehensive programme of improvements, accessibility will be enhanced and is expected to act as a benchmark for what can be achieved in an historic building. (Photo: © CL-Median/Shutterstock.com)

OPPOSITE: Kings Cross Station, London. (Photo: © digitalwhiz/Adobe Stock)

to be in the vanguard in providing accessible buildings and environments. As a minimum, they should meet current legislative requirements and preferably demonstrate best practice. Guardians of such buildings will wish to retain their historic significance while demonstrating a commitment to equality of access.

Most government buildings will have been altered extensively over the years. The oldest, which may well have been constructed prior to the introduction of electricity, will definitely have been adapted. In addition, many will have been adapted to allow for the easy transfer of post and other office supplies as well as for limited movement of staff and visitors.

In aspiring to achieve the highest standards, the government sets a benchmark for others, in the UK and elsewhere. Many countries without prescriptive legislation in place now adopt UK standards and best practice in recognition of the progress the UK has made in providing inclusive design.

The Supreme Court of Justice and the Treasury are just two significant government buildings that illustrate the improvements that can be made in highly public institutions, as well as in buildings that provide little public access. In both cases, all occupants benefit from the inclusive improvements.

Galleries and Museums

Many of our well-loved galleries and museums are located in protected, historic buildings. These might range from the earliest purpose-built galleries, such as the north wing of Somerset House, designed to incorporate the Royal Academy and now housing the Courtauld, to the modernist De la Warr pavilion in Bexhill.

The contribution of galleries and museums to both civic pride and the economy has led to significant investment in recent years. Such investment has resulted not only in improved physical access, but also to significant changes in the way objects are displayed and interpreted. Such changes, as well as the growing availability of computerized equipment, have contributed to the growing popularity of

galleries and museums. Commentaries, presented by experts in their field, can enhance the enjoyment and understanding of all, as can devices that allow visitors to display accompanying text in a font size that suits. Policies that allow visitors to touch and even pick up objects mean that one does not always have to be able to see a piece of art in order to appreciate it.

The spending power of the ageing population means that access improvements can result in further advantages as money is spent in the café or bookshop. Thus, it pays to invest in step-free or easy access, as well as in clear signage and good WC facilities.

Tate Britain and Tate Modern, the Natural History Museum and the Soane Museum, all housed in buildings of historic significance, illustrate improvements that can be made for the benefit of all while retaining and even enhancing the significance of the historic fabric.

Transport

Government policy is increasingly focused on the benefits of using public transport as opposed to the private car. Transport providers are responding by making transport systems, connections and

The front entrance steps to the Natural History Museum have long been a formidable obstacle to accessibility, not least those on the final approach to the main entrance. These steps have been modified by introducing a ramped slope to each side, thereby benefitting wheelchair users and also the many parents who visit with their children and buggies.

interchanges readily accessible to everyone, including disabled and older passengers.

Work on transport facilities will usually have an impact on the surrounding public realm. The effective provision of high quality access requires a holistic approach, ranging from the location of parking and taxi set-down to the detailed design of wayfinding and safety measures. A range of guidance is available, such as the Department for Transport's Code of Practice Accessible Train Station Design for Disabled People (2011), and other relevant information on best practice.

Most of our railway stations were built by the Victorians long before the advent of any campaign for accessible design. Today, however, the popularity of rail travel, the preponderance of children's buggies and the invention of suitcases with wheels, have all encouraged the rail industry to invest in inclusive design.

At most stations, and especially our larger transport interchanges, the importance of clear signage and distinct announcements for the efficient transfer of passengers has long been recognized. London Transport introduced a signage policy early in the twentieth century. Similarly, the entire rail network uses uniform signage that is both clear and familiar. The importance of clear announcements is essential, and although quality might vary, the determination to ensure that all passengers can follow signage and hear important announcements is of particular benefit to those with vision and hearing impairments.

Furthermore, the requirement to keep travellers moving quickly encourages rail staff to eliminate obstacles where possible, while safety concerns ensure that the edges of platforms as well as other hazards are clearly 'signposted'.

In stations, it is often those with mobility rather than sensory limitations who face the greatest impediments. Train stations were designed before the advent of lifts and escalators and porters were usually employed to carry luggage, so little heed was paid to the provision of step-free routes. The investment in rail infrastructure over recent decades has changed this, with the insertion of lifts and escalators in many of our busiest stations. This is complemented

Most major railway stations in the UK were built in the Victorian period. Here at Kings Cross Station in London, passengers can now move seamlessly from the street onto all platforms without using steps. (Photo: (c) asiastock/shutterstock.com)

by management changes that have led to the provision of powered vehicles for those unable to walk long distances, and portable ramps, which enable wheelchair users, with assistance, to enter their train carriage.

This work has been carried out in some of our most loved and historically significant stations, involving thoughtful input from a variety of stakeholders, ranging from rail infrastructure specialists and train operators to conservation specialists and passenger groups. The Grade 1 listed Kings Cross Station, as well as Cannon Street and London Bridge, are three London interchanges that have benefitted from significant investment with a range of improvements that are now benefitting all travellers.

Theatres and Concert Halls

Most of our cities and larger towns will have a theatre, playhouse or concert hall, often a much loved venue where children might enjoy their first pantomime and teenagers their first pop concert. The auditorium will be used for a range of activities, from serious ballet and theatre to conferences and degree day ceremonies.

London's West End has the highest concentration of theatres anywhere in the world. The theatre district attracts around 12 million visitors each year and contributes around £1 billion to the UK economy.

The major upgrade of the Royal Shakespeare Theatre in Stratford-upon-Avon provided a significant opportunity to comprehensively improve access for disabled theatregoers. This not only allowed for step-free routes to all parts of the theatre, it also made innovative improvements for the means of escape using lifts. (Photo: trabantos/Shutterstock.com)

The importance of theatres and other places of entertainment to both civic pride and to the economy have resulted in significant investment in recent years, a strategy that is likely to continue. Such investment provides the opportunity to improve access for audience and performers, an aim that is of particular significance as theatre managers recognize the importance of the 'grey pound' in sustaining box office success.

The majority of the country's theatres are Victorian or Edwardian, built at a time when there was little ambition to provide access for all. These theatres, many of them listed, are frequently in need of upgrading to address repair backlogs, to embrace modern technologies and to meet audience expectations. By considering creative and innovative solutions, it is possible to balance the requirements of access legislation with the desire to respect the historic fabric. Success in this specialized area benefits from close liaison with approvals authorities at both local and national level.

Access improvements in such places of entertainment might range from providing useful information on the website, such as the location of the nearest step-free train station or Blue Badge parking bay, to the location of wheelchair and easy access seating. Successful adaptations include the Royal Shakespeare Theatre in Stratford-on-Avon, the Hackney Empire and the Opera House in London's Covent Garden.

Universities

Many universities have a number of historic buildings within their portfolio. In line with conservation best practice, it pays to adopt a systematic approach to improving access, based on a detailed understanding of the historic significance of the building and its wider campus.

Educational institutions are increasingly concerned about accessibility issues in the light of changing policy and legislation. With rising expectations, colleges are more aware of their reputations and the need to provide equality of access. This applies not only to students and staff but also to the visiting public. The availability of college facilities for events and conferences is a growing business for universities.

The dining room at Mansell College, Oxford, to the right of the entrance tower, is up a difficult flight of stairs. This obstacle to accessibility has been overcome by the discreet insertion of a lift and the provision of an accessible WC.

To meet expectations, but also to maximize opportunities, facilities need to be accessible.

Fundamental to a successful campus is its landscape and the spaces between buildings. These areas and how they are used may be overlooked in favour of the focus on individual buildings. When considering access it helps to adopt a wider strategic view, looking at circulation, wayfinding, safety, transport and operational issues that may affect the delivery and experience of educational services.

The preparation of a campus-wide access audit that records current provision that exists on campus relative to reasonable expectations is an invaluable way to start the process of improving access. The audit will generate a list of priorities within the context of any longer-term objectives for an individual building or the campus as a whole. Longer-term recommendations can then be incorporated into estate improvement plans as funding and opportunities allow.

Hotels

Businesses are increasingly aware of the impact that meeting access legislation can have on their reputations. A hotel's success will depend, in part, upon its ability to provide flexible accommodation that is suitable for all visitors. The concept of inclusive design means that, in most instances, specialist provision for people with disabilities is not required. Instead, it forms part of a hotel's standard arrangements.

Hotels will incorporate some elements that are of particular use to people with disabilities – these may include larger showers for wheelchair users or pillows that vibrate if a fire alarm is triggered, for visitors who are deaf. It is essential that hotel staff have appropriate training so that they know of the availability of these provisions and are able to discuss, sensitively, the particular needs of the visitor.

Leisure

Access to sport and leisure facilities for personal enjoyment and for well-being is becoming an increasingly significant element of the nation's recreational activity. Providers of leisure facilities are mindful of the need for inclusive access, as well as how effectively they respond to social expectations and business opportunities. A facility's reputation will depend, in part, on how accessible it is perceived to be in relation to the Equality Act 2010.

Achieving accessibility contributes to the success of recreational buildings by ensuring that they welcome a wider audience that will include older people, visitors with children and people with disabilities. It is important that visitors to a venue experience no obstacle in entering the building, buying tickets and enjoying the pool, the gym or the basketball court. It is a premise of inclusive design that it achieves its purpose unobtrusively. Ease of access may be due, in large part, to the fact that the venue was designed to meet the requirements of disabled people, but this need not be obvious to any visitor. A clear example of this is the Ironmonger Row Swimming Baths in north London. Built to provide washing, laundering and swimming facilities for local residents in the early twentieth century, these Grade ll listed baths were initially adapted when Turkish Bath facilities were added. More recently, they were upgraded to provide full access.

Shops and Offices

Developers, landlords and tenants are increasingly aware of the need for inclusive access for both the public and employees. Building values and a development's marketability can depend, in part, on how accessible a building is, in relation to both current and emerging standards. Tenants and landlords will be concerned to know whether the development they are considering meets their obligations under the Equality Act 2010. Carrying out an access audit can highlight deficiencies and help facilities managers to develop a programme of access improvements. It often helps to do this with staff representatives to ensure effective consultation and productive discussion. As is often the case, consultation at an early design stage will provide the best outcome, enhancing project values and business potential. Again, many of our most valued stores are located in listed buildings, such as the Grade ll* Peter Jones in Sloane Square.

Places of Worship

Places of worship are frequently located in much loved buildings in historic locations. Although the religious community will want to have an accessible building, it may be of concern that any adaptations involved will adversely intrude upon the spirit of the place. It will want to ensure that proposed interventions retain the aura of the setting while ensuring that the building and its grounds are more usable by all.

The Church of St Bartholomew the Great in the City of London is approached by a level path at street level. This provides step-free access into the church not just for visitors but also for the many older and disabled parishioners. (Photo: Kiev.Victor/Shutterstock.com)

Places of worship often offer other facilities and activities, including playgroups, lunch clubs and community meeting spaces. The users of these will also expect effective access arrangements. Improved access is in particular demand for larger cathedrals and abbeys offering information and services to large numbers of visitors. Access for older and disabled people, as well as parents with small children, can play a key role in the success of any 'visitor offer' business plan.

Successful interventions have contributed significantly and been welcomed by worshippers. Peterborough Cathedral, Friends House and many local parish churches, such as St Bartholomew the Great in Smithfield and St Giles nearby, are cases in point.

Housing

Government and local authority planning policies promote the value of inclusive design in housing of all tenures. The general wish of most disabled residents, supported by government policy, is for adaptable mainstream housing rather than special needs accommodation. This acceptance by government represented a breakthrough in thinking and is increasingly being achieved in projects such as the award-winning Adelaide Wharf. It is a key feature of The Olympic Village, now East Village, across all types and tenures of accommodation provided. Historic examples will mostly be almshouses, purpose-designed in their day for frail and older people. These were not always notable for their accessibility but over time have had to change.

Public Realm

Enjoyment of the public realm, whether in small towns or large cities, is an important element of our day to day experience. In recent years there has been increased investment in the public realm, in recognition of its contribution to a sense of well-being and its importance in attracting visitors from both the UK and abroad.

Hand in hand with this investment has been a growing appreciation of the importance of inclusive design to benefit all, whether people with disabilities, parents with buggies or tourists with suitcases. This shift of priorities, away from vehicles and instead to pedestrians, has demanded fresh thinking of how we negotiate the public realm, be it a local neighbourhood or a city centre.

When improvement schemes are carried out on the approach to an historic building, or in a conservation area, it is important that they enhance rather than detract from the special interest of the setting. Although we have all been exasperated by the addition of ramps or pavings that jar aesthetically, or by notices telling wheelchair users to use a back entrance, there are now numerous examples of high quality, non-slip paving, imperceptible slopes, attractive, clear signage and welcoming ramps that improve access for all.

Enjoyment of our outdoor spaces, whether in a country park or city centre, is increasingly recognized as an important aspect of modern life. Strategic thinking will help to address the potentially competing demands of heritage, culture and inclusive design in extensive landscaped areas or in historic parkland. With large landscape projects, it can help to concentrate efforts in the areas of maximum use or popularity. An initial access audit of existing spaces and attractions will reveal how they are used and will help in prioritizing options.

Public realm projects benefit hugely from access-specific consultation with the local community by employing techniques that encourage meaningful and effective input from the outset. Designing an inclusive environment requires consideration of all needs, including mobility, sensory and intellectual. Some requirements may be in competition. For example, guide dogs are trained to identify kerbs as places to halt, while wheelchair users may prefer kerb-free footpaths. Such issues are not insurmountable and thoughtful design, backed up by research, can result in effective solutions that satisfy all.

Windsor Great Park, London's South Bank and Exhibition Road in Kensington provide examples of high quality design that has emerged out of a clear strategy and extensive consultation.

Exhibition Road serves the entrances of several important national museums. Before the road was altered by the introduction of a single surface, an extensive consultation process was undertaken. This photograph shows the early conceptual idea marked out on the road to gauge public reaction to the proposals.

The Future

Every type of historic building, from medieval cathedral to modernist art gallery, has been changed over its lifetime. Initially, this might have been to add electricity or to incorporate toilets. More recently, as we have seen, the provision of improved access may have forced the pace of change. Such changes, which may initially have been resisted, are now embraced by owners, management boards, funding organizations and conservationists. It has been recognized that the provision of good access can benefit all who use a building or enjoy the spaces around it.

In the past, change may have been resisted, sometimes with good cause. We have all seen cumbersome ramps, unsightly platform lifts or unsympathetic signage added to a building we love. However, the burgeoning of access adaptations over the last quarter of a century has resulted in clients who are more discerning and a design profession that has embraced the creative opportunities presented by the challenge. We can now enjoy a range of adaptations; some are discreet, some are bold, most are sensitive and many are ingenious. The case studies that follow will demonstrate a range of solutions each suited to the building, its use and its location.

Chapter Three

Methodology

Legislation

In 1995 the Disability Discrimination Act became law and presented the design and construction industry with a challenge. It required owners or custodians of all buildings offering a service to the public to make reasonable adjustments in order that the service could be accessed by disabled people. There were a few exemptions to this, but not on the grounds of being listed as an historic building.

To a large extent the industry was unprepared, but the legislation anticipated this by moving forward in three phases, each within a fixed period of time, and with an ultimate deadline for compliance of ten years. This was both practical and helpful, allowing time for professionals to respond thoughtfully. It enabled the legislative objectives to be widely published and for practical guidance to become available. Progress was monitored under the watchful eye of a Disability Rights Commission set up for the purpose.

The Strategy

The underlying aim was to ensure that the 'service' could be provided. Therefore, the first consideration (Phase 1) was to review building management policy. Did the building policy, even inadvertently, prevent disabled people from using the service on offer? An example regularly cited at the time was the widely prevailing policy of prohibiting dogs from entering public buildings, especially restaurants. This arose for all sorts of health reasons, but might the policy be reasonably modified to make an exemption for guide dogs? If so, the problem could readily be solved by modifying the policy.

The second consideration (Phase 2) was to review the scope for making use of assistive technology. It quickly spawned a new industry, especially in the world of arts and entertainment where blind and deaf people were often unable to enjoy a play or an exhibition. For example, in theatres, assistive

The diagram shows the three phases for implementing reasonable adjustments as set out in the 1995 legislation.

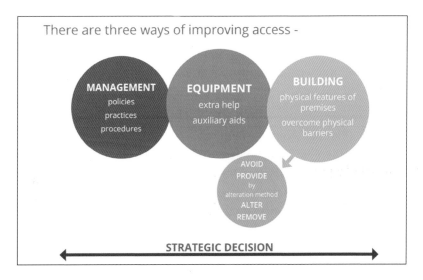

There are three ways of improving access –

MANAGEMENT
policies
practices
procedures

EQUIPMENT
extra help
auxiliary aids

BUILDING
physical features of premises
overcome physical barriers

AVOID
PROVIDE
by alteration method
ALTER
REMOVE

STRATEGIC DECISION

OPPOSITE: Tate Britain on London's Millbank. (Photo: Rept0n1x, CC BY-SA 3, via Wikimedia Commons)

hearing devices for people with hearing impairments or pre-recorded descriptions of plays (programmes) for blind and partially sighted people soon became available. Or, more simply, it might mean the installation of a handrail to a staircase or the addition of steps or the creation of a ramp in a stepped corridor.

And finally (Phase 3), where the above were insufficient to achieve 'reasonable access to the service', the building itself might need to be altered to overcome the obstacle. This might involve altering or relocating a front entrance or installing a lift.

All the above might reasonably apply to any building offering a service to the public regardless of whether it was an historic building or not. Museums, galleries and theatres, often historic buildings, came squarely within the remit of the legislation. Guidance was urgently required by those responsible for the conservation of historic buildings on how the new challenge could be met. On the one hand, conservationists already had a duty to 'conserve'; how, then, was that obligation going to be reconciled with the new duty to provide access?

Regulations

The UK building regulations strike a careful balance between the need for accessibility and the need for conservation. The section that refers to historic buildings makes clear that:

> They are a finite resource with cultural importance ... The aim should be to improve accessibility where and to the extent that it is practically possible, always provided that the work does not prejudice the character of the historic building, or increase the risk of long term deterioration of the building fabric.

Approved Document Part M General Guidance, para 0.18 p.13

Essentially, the regulations are concerned that practical measures for safety should be in place, especially for people with impaired vision or poor balance. This concern will apply as much to the outside of the building as inside, particularly with regard to approach paths, steps and ramps. From the turn of the new millennium, experience has shown that there are discreet ways to improve external surfaces, even cobbles and granite setts. Inside the building, good judgement will need to be relied on with the balance always towards retaining historic interiors rather than changing them. For example, it often benefits both safety and conservation to apply a protective covering, like a carpet runner, to fragile floor surfaces. Similarly, assistance from staff or volunteers, especially as guides, will help offset the need to introduce signage.

Guidance

Among the early publications of importance was one published by English Heritage, now Heritage England, entitled, *Easy Access to Historic Buildings*. It was a breakthrough in thinking for those concerned with building conservation on how an acceptable response to physical change might be assessed. The starting point of the guidance was to undertake not only a conservation study but also an access audit.

Funding

The new Disability Discrimination Act legislation immediately raised the issue of funding. Who would pay for the improvements required, varying in scale from minor works to major, with costs to match? The burden of cost rested in most cases with the building owner, thus representing an unwelcome responsibility for historic building owners already faced with maintenance and repair bills.

The original publication of 1995.

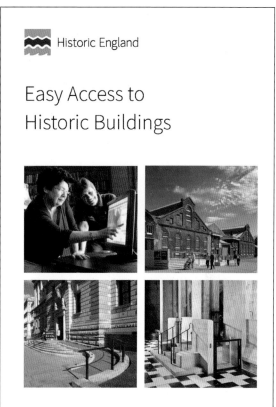

The latest version published in 2015.

In the UK both the HLF and Arts Council England (ACE) responded. Both of these public institutions allocated funding to projects aimed at improving historic buildings. A condition of that funding was now to demonstrate that improved accessibility would be achieved as part of any general improvements programme. This proved to be an effective carrot and stick approach applied rigorously by ACE who went so far as to develop their own access guidelines and encourage consultation with disabled building 'users'. The professions had to respond, leading to the emergence of access consultancy as a key player in influencing design decisions and presenting convincing information for funders to assess.

Assessing the Scope for Change

Almost any existing building will be under pressure to change when altered circumstances arise. Historic buildings open to the public are no exception, though the scope for change will be additionally restricted by concerns for conservation. However, assessing any need for change to meet current expectations for accessibility is an obligation and begins by undertaking an access audit. This helps by mapping out key areas of the building where obstacles to accessibility are critical.

The conservation plan maps out the historic status of the building fabric and is an aid to knowing where change might and might not be possible. It is

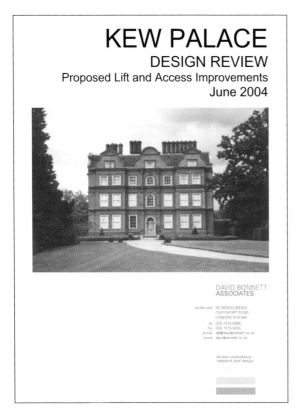

KEW PALACE
DESIGN REVIEW
Proposed Lift and Access Improvements
June 2004

DAVID BONNETT
ASSOCIATES

studio one 32 INDIGO MEWS
CARYSFORT ROAD
LONDON N16 9AE
tel 020 7275 0065
fax 020 7275 9035
e-mail db@davidbonnett.co.uk
www davidbonnett.co.uk

access consultancy
research and design

A typical access review where recommendations are 'tested'
against the conservation plan findings.

important to review the access audit alongside the
findings of the conservation plan.

Comparative Method

With this information to hand, the options for improving accessibility can be systematically reviewed. At
this point, the design team might usefully look at
comparative examples elsewhere in the UK developed over the last twenty-five years. The following
do precisely that by examining a selected sample of
case studies and also by looking at these case studies
as typologies. These are shown here as diagrams,
each representing in principle the type of solution
or solutions applied, since there are often two and
sometimes more. The diagrams are kept simple in
order to capture the essence of the idea.

Modification, Including Repositioning

Most historic buildings were constructed using relatively simple techniques employing timber, brick and
stone. The relevance of this point is that a simply built
component such as entrance steps might be carefully
taken apart and then reassembled in a new position.

Such was the case at Kew Palace in Kew Gardens.
Here, the front steps were an obstacle to access and a
resolution was needed in order to provide step-free
access, but with a minimum of visual change to its
symmetrical elevation. To achieve this, the original
steps were carefully taken apart and reassembled on
the same axis but pulled forward just sufficient to
discretely insert a shallow ramp. The change is barely
perceptible on approach to the building, thereby
addressing real concerns for conservation.

In another example, at the Treasury in London, the
original steps were replaced and pulled forward, as with
Kew, to allow the insertion of a symmetrical ramp. This
certainly resolved the inaccessibility of this entrance and
has arguably improved the appearance of the building.

Modification sketch.

The original front steps at Kew Palace have been repositioned to provide a new landing. The ramp to the landing is on the right and, as intended, can barely be noticed on approach. (Photo: Afflamen/ Shutterstock.com)

At the Treasury the original entrance step location has been repositioned forward sufficient to provide a landing. In this case the ramp is symmetrically positioned on each side, making a visual statement.

Addition/Extension

This refers to the construction of an adjoining structure or sometimes the acquisition of an adjoining property, located alongside the historic building. Rather than unacceptably altering the historic building by the addition of level entrances, lifts, and so on, these are instead provided within the new or neighbouring structure that, in turn, connects to the old.

A classic example of this is the Roundhouse in north London, originally designed as a huge revolving turntable for steam trains constructed using an early cast

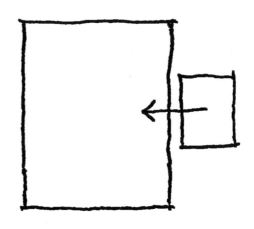

Addition/Extension sketch.

iron frame clad in brick and roofed in slate. A strategic decision was made at an early stage that the visually striking round shape of the building should not be disturbed. Instead the new elements, including a lift, WC facilities, café and more were all housed in a new addition. This, in turn, connects to the old by means of a dramatic glazed link housing a grand staircase and acting as a beacon to passers-by, especially at night.

The Roundhouse with its new addition to the right incorporating visitor facilities, including access lift, WCs and a café.

Whitechapel Art Gallery to the left of Aldgate East Station entrance, and its neighbouring library building on the right. When library building was purchased by the gallery, the two buildings were connected and a shared lift installed.

Another example is the Whitechapel Art Gallery, also in north London, designed as a gallery from the outset in 1901, but as is so often the case, increased public use led to increased expectations such that funding was sought for major internal improvements. Inescapably, these included better accessibility. By good fortune, its immediate neighbour, itself a listed library building, became available for acquisition. It was therefore an 'addition', giving rise to a variety of options of how the two adjoining buildings would connect to mutual benefit. This included the key introduction of a lift connecting all floor levels of the adjoining buildings.

Insertion

As the name suggests, this term implies identifying a key location within an historic building where a lift might be inserted in order to provide step-free access to other floor levels. The 'insertion' may be part of a wider range of changes, but once the location of the lift has been agreed in principle, most other considerations then fall into place.

An example is Queens House Greenwich, where the conservation study revealed that a servants' staircase had been replaced several times throughout the history of the building. This raised the option of replacing the staircase once again, but reducing it in

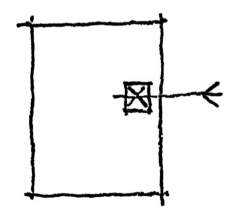

Insertion sketch.

The gallery at Queens House and the entrance hall below are both now accessed by lift inserted in the undercroft below.

Behind this bookcase in the Soane Museum is a new lift serving all levels. It is inserted into the space once occupied by closets on each level. (©Dennis Gilbert/VIEW)

size, thereby providing sufficient additional space in the stairwell for a lift to be installed. This key decision influenced how the public might enter and circulate within the building in its new role as a Museum of Time. Critically, the lift location must 'work' on each of the floor levels that are served and here some degree of compromise might be called for.

A service stair connecting all floor levels is, of course, ideal, but a similar situation can arise where other types of service spaces are located, one above the other. Original plans of the Sir John Soane's Museum in London show its original closets behind the main staircase, long since used as storage cupboards. The closet locations and their size provided just sufficient 'footprint' for a small passenger lift to be installed. The new lift is necessarily small, but acceptable if a special wheelchair is used. This wheelchair is sufficiently narrow not only for lift access but also for the narrow circulation corridors.

Reorientation

It is often the case that the main entrance of an historic public building is up a flight of steps. Tate Britain on the north bank of the Thames is one such example. Here, the steps are such an integral part of

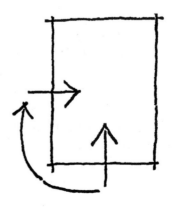

Reorientation sketch.

The new ramped entrance to Tate Britain reorients the entrance from the front of the building to the side.

The new ramp to Christ Church undercroft at Spitalfields avoids the famous, but forbidding, front steps.

the building frontage, and an obstacle to access, that any effective change would be almost inconceivable.

In these situations it is worth considering reorientating the entrance to a less imposing elevation that can accommodate a new building element, in this case a ramp. According to each circumstance, the ramp might go up or it might go down as at Tate Britain. To enable such an option to work it must make sense with regard to the internal circulation routes and add value to the project as a whole. At Tate Britain this was precisely the case, with a reorientated entrance made possible with a ramp. It provides direct and a more logical entry into the rearranged gallery complex, with a new lift and visitor WCs close by.

A further example is the new ramped entry into Christ Church in Spitalfields. As with Tate Britain, the frontage steps are a robust, vital part of the building frontage and, as such, confound all change. So, the idea of reorientating the entrance to the side of the building was explored, leaving the all-important front elevation untouched. The new side entrance and ramp direct visitors down into the crypt below the main

church where community and visitor facilities are provided, including a lift up to the main church level.

Mechanization

In the earlier years of inclusive design, there was a keen interest in the potential for mechanical devices to overcome the obstacles presented by entrance steps. The thinking then was that a mechanical solution, such as a platform lift, would avoid the cost and disruption of physical alterations to an historic building.

The choice of devices available was limited and so too the height that a wheelchair could be lifted. Furthermore, the devices were engineering solutions with little attempt to refine their appearance. The initial enthusiasm for this type of equipment faded and was directed instead towards the ramp. They could be made to look beautiful and, of course, reliability of use was assured.

However, there remain instances where space for a ramp simply does not exist, or the height to be

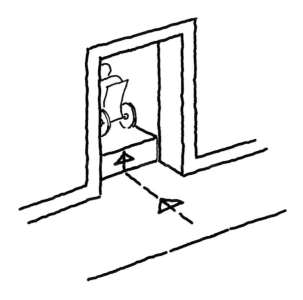

Mechanization sketch.

for a ramp on the pavement. Instead, a new lift was installed on the internal face of the building and a lift door specially cut through the original stonework. The reliability of lifts has improved, and in addition to this welcome change, a new type of lift has been developed that relies on hydraulic pumps. This has opened up new possibilities. These lifts allow the original steps to 'stay' in place, moving only when required to convey a wheelchair user into the building.

At the Supreme Court the entrance is at pavement level but with several steps beyond in the foyer. For this reason, two platform lifts have been installed either side of the internal steps to provide step-free access. (Photo: © chris2766/Adobe Stock)

overcome is simply too much to be practical. In these cases, recent improvements in lifting capability and the appearance of lifts have widened the choice on offer, with the option of clothing them to suit the building they serve. At the visitor entrance to the Treasury in Whitehall, there was insufficient room

At the Treasury the existing stepped entrance remains unchanged. On the right is the new lift accessed directly from pavement level. Note how an opening has been cut through the original stonework for this purpose.

Chapter Four

Elements for Accessibility

WHEN EMBARKING ON AN ACCESS appraisal it is essential to consider the principal elements of accessibility from the outset. What is it that is being aimed for? The underlying aim is to enable everyone, regardless of disability, to enter the building in question, make use of its facilities and then leave safely, including in an emergency. Use of the building will rely on a list of accessibility features familiar to everyone.

There was no exemption for historic buildings from the Disability Discrimination Act 1995 where the building offered a service to the public.

OPPOSITE: Peterborough Cathedral, West frontage. (Photo: © Smolik. sm/Adobe Stock)

Ideally, accessibility – let us call it that – should be possible throughout, and compromise or short measures should not be entertained until all options have been examined. Three tools for the appraisal process are helpful: first, a basic checklist of aims; this, along with diagrams, assist with understanding. Second, an available set of plans that can be coloured up by hand. Finally, the conservation plan of your building. Keep this close by for reference.

When reviewing the checklist it is important to understand that you are appraising a 'visitor journey' that must work as a whole if accessibility is to be achieved. This might be envisaged as a linked chain; any break in the chain, just one, could undermine the visitor journey experience. It is also helpful to understand that any limitation becomes more acceptable to the visitor if it is offset by a benefit.

It is commonly the case that proposals for improved accessibility are part of a wider programme of improvements. This can prove advantageous where altered structures and services are anticipated.

Arrival

Arrival in an urban area is frequently by public transport, and building staff and local people will be familiar with local public transport availability, such as trains and buses that provide access to the venue. This availability should be described on any pre-visit information, noting also the location of the train and bus stations and the bus stops and their distance from the building to be visited. It will also be necessary to check to see if parking is unrestricted or if Disabled Blue Badge parking spaces are close by, either by physically checking or by asking the

Arrival sketch.

local authority, which keeps a list of locations. Then check if a taxi might, without restriction, set down passengers outside or close by the building. Bus lanes may prevent this, so too bike lanes. When describing the means of arrival, note the location of pedestrian crossings that will need to form part of the journey to and from the building.

In rural locations, visitor arrival will almost certainly be by car, inevitably with the need for visitors to rely on either street parking in the locality or, more probably, on on-site car parking. If the latter, the parking may well be some distance from the building entrance, to ensure that the building and its approaches are not cluttered up by the visual distraction of parked vehicles.

For this reason, it is often the case that parking is some distance away, too far perhaps for some people to manage. If so, consider the use of a people carrier – usually a battery-powered 'buggy' of the type used in larger rail stations. This will, of course, have

The visitor car park for Kew Palace is a considerable distance from the palace itself. (Photo: © Elena Rostunova/Dreamstime.com)

An accessible buggy like this can resolve such problems if justified by high visitor numbers. (Photo: Gary Perkin/ Shutterstock.com)

implications for costs, both capital and revenue, but such costs might be managed through sponsorship.

Any on-site parking should include the provision of some parking bays designated for use by disabled visitors. Ideally, these should be as near as possible to the building entrance.

Approach

Getting from an arrival point, usually the public highway, to the building entrance may be the first problem encountered. This is less likely to be the case in urban settings where the public pavement is used, but it is quite likely in rural settings where an approach path over a distance might be unavoidable.

Gradients and approach paths can usually be modified in some way, but distances cannot be shrunk. The difficulty of distance, if an issue, might be mitigated by the introduction of rest points. At its simplest, a rest point might be a bench seat or, more elaborately, a shelter with directional signage, information and a map.

Of all the elements making up an historic building, the external areas are those most likely to have changed over the years. The conservation plan should establish the facts. A cobbled path, unsuitable for

Approach sketch.

comfortable walking, may look old but might have been laid or relaid in recent years. This offers scope for change or at least modification of part of the surface.

Avoid, if possible, an approach route for disabled visitors that significantly deviates from the route

This approach path is a considerable distance to walk with no obvious place to rest.

The introduction of seating to enable people to rest can helpfully mitigate distances and if thoughtfully designed and located, will add to the visitor experience.

used by others. Such routes often involve controlled entry leading to confusion, which is not the best way to begin the visitor journey.

Entry

How an historic building is entered can set the tone for the whole visitor experience that follows. An uplifting experience shared with family and friends is the ideal, especially if there is a 'wow' moment at the point of entry. A more distant or inconvenient entrance may have the opposite effect, particularly if special arrangements are required involving waiting, perhaps to unlock a side door for wheelchair access.

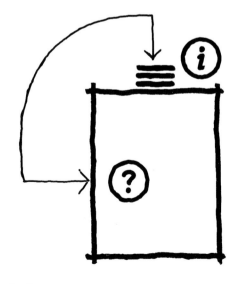

Entry sketch.

At the Supreme Court in London, visitors have to use a platform lift, but it is within the main visitor entrance lobby and in full view of staff who may need to assist. By comparison, its near neighbour, the Treasury, has a platform lift accessed from the street, out of the view of staff and dependent on them responding to a call button when pressed. With highly trained staff as at the Treasury, this is rarely a problem, but where resources are under pressure, it may create difficulties.

Ideally, a building entrance should be designed to ensure that disabled visitors are not separated from friends and family, but instead is easily used by all. This is successfully achieved at the V&A Museum of Childhood where the original entrance steps have been replaced by a gentle gradient that allows parents and children easy access without steps. The frontage area should provide that 'wow' moment for those arriving at the museum, and not the immediate concern about how to enter if in a

At the Museum of Childhood, the front entrance has been transformed by the replacement of the original steps by a gradient which, by design, provides a wonderful play area for children. (Photo: Helene Binet)

The new entrance, beneath the stair, at Queen's House serves all visitors, replacing the original arrangement where wheelchair users were separated on arrival from family and friends.

wheelchair or negotiating with a buggy. Similarly, at the Queen's House Greenwich the original ramp at the rear of the building served as a separate entrance for wheelchair users, while their family and friends used the steps. This arrangement has now changed, with the introduction of a single step-free entrance for everyone.

Information/Communication

Venue websites are now anticipated for even the most modest building and they help visitors with advance planning. Once at the venue, visitors may require further information, so a practical solution would be to have a staffed reception/information desk, especially in historic buildings where physical alterations may need to be minimized. Reception/information desks are certainly essential for larger buildings where ticketing is in place or where guided tours are part of the visitor experience. However, staff, and even volunteers, cost money and need to be efficiently distributed at key locations, most particularly on entry.

The term 'aids to communications' typically refers to measures that will help people with impaired hearing or sight to get the best possible experience from a building. These measures are invariably reliant on equipment installed or made available, for example, at a visitor reception desk on arrival in the same manner as printed visitor guides and information wands. It should be remembered that any equipment will usually require some basic training for staff and routine testing and maintenance.

As the size and complexity of a building increases so will the need for this type of equipment, especially if lecture halls and conference facilities are available. Furthermore, this kind of equipment will be required not just for conference attendees but for presenters too who may have similar needs.

Museums and galleries in the UK have gained considerable experience in communications technology and how it is best made available and applied, regardless of whether or not the venue is a listed building. The same is the case for transport interchanges where public announcement systems and other means of communication are critical to efficiency as much as to convenience.

Rarely should the installation of this type of equipment need to impact detrimentally on the character of an historic building. If it does, it is more likely the result of clumsy surface wiring or thoughtless workmanship rather than an inevitable consequence of the installation.

Initial enquiries concerning accessibility to an historic building will usually rely on a visitor website. (Photo: BongKarnGraphic/ Shutterstock.com)

Clear and effective directional signage is essential inside buildings, particularly those that are more complex.

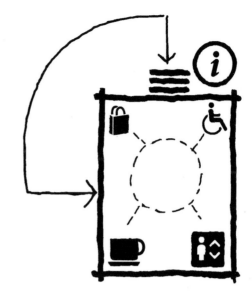

Circulation sketch.

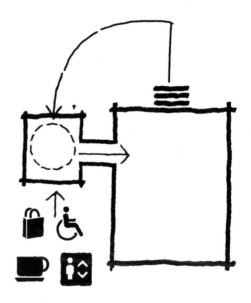

Sometimes the choice may be to incorporate key visitor facilities in a new extension building rather than in the main building itself. The primary access route is shown as being within the building on the upper diagram, but within a new extension in the lower diagram.

Circulation

When moving around is difficult, a clearly signed and convenient circulation route will enable the visitor to get the best from a day's visit. By contrast, going the 'wrong way' and then having to retrace one's steps will be disappointing. Any time-limited journey is best planned and even more so if personal energy levels are limited.

Every effort should therefore be made, at the outset, to create a logical and convenient route that connects all key facilities. This is referred to as the primary access route and every effort must be made to meet expectations. Typically, key facilities will include a reception/arrival point, WC facilities, lifts/ stairs, café and shop. For this reason, these elements are often successfully provided in a separate extension connected to the historic building rather than within it. The Roundhouse in London is an example and so too is the Garden Museum, with its new restaurant, meeting rooms and toilet facilities.

Thereafter, the circulation route will be determined in large part by the historic building itself and the spaces to be visited. Since all historic buildings

The exceptionally restrictive corridors at the Soane Museum require visitors to use a special narrow wheelchair.

If too narrow, they prevent wheelchair users from passing through, and if too heavy they will inhibit access for able-bodied and disabled alike.

Little can be done to widen an historic door opening without the potential for irreversible damage. Instead, either an alternative, wider entrance might be found or a narrower wheelchair could be provided. Identifying an alternative entrance will be part of any typical access appraisal. Opting to use a narrow wheelchair is uncommon, but does occur in special circumstances. The Sir John Soane's Museum in London is an example of where a special wheelchair is used. Here, the visitor passes through otherwise inaccessible corridors and permanent display areas. The 'trade-off' is that the wheelchair is pushed by a well-informed staff member, who provides a personal guided tour.

are different, this will vary, but the focus here is on the fabric of the building, not necessarily the displays within them. Displays might be moveable but the historic building fabric is not. This is the stage for planning the secondary access route, that is, a route that makes the best of what is available. Comprehensive access may not be possible initially, leading to disappointment, but this may have to be accepted, at least until a later date. In time, new technologies may mitigate disappointment by enabling the space – a beautifully decorated room perhaps in a difficult location – to, at least, be 'seen' virtually.

Doors

The suitability of doors for accessibility is largely determined by their width, but also by their weight.

At Christ Church Spitalfields, power-operated inner doors have been installed to provide protection from the weather.

Overcoming the limitations of heavy doors may be addressed in a variety of ways, the most obvious being, if possible, to leave the door open during visiting hours. If it is an external door, suitable new inner doors can be installed to provide protection from the weather. Alternatively, the heavy door can be managed, that is, opened and closed by a staff member when required. However, power operation of the door should be considered, involving minor but reversible alterations. The costs of this type of installation must include ongoing maintenance as well as installation.

Levels

A change in levels refers to anything from a single step in a corridor to the need to move between upper and lower floor levels. Resolving the challenges of level changes is part of the skills set required for improving accessibility.

Avoiding a step or steps may be possible by finding or creating an alternative route. If this contributes to a coherent general circulation route, then this is ideal. However, if it creates a 'disabled access' side route it may be preferable to convert the step(s) into a ramp instead. Such changes often have the advantage of being reversible.

The use of portable ramps is less attractive as a solution but not out of the question if they provide access where otherwise there would be none. Portable ramps can be heavy and will impose on staff who will need to erect them and then stow them away. But in the final analysis, if the space or place to be visited is of real interest to the visitor, some compromise or inconvenience will usually be accepted. The design and construction of ramps, even temporary ones, must take safety into account, with handrails for support securely fixed and ramp surfaces ideally slip-resistant.

Moving between floor levels by inserting a lift will be one of the more ambitious changes likely to be considered in an historic building. Examples are covered in the later case studies. Their location will

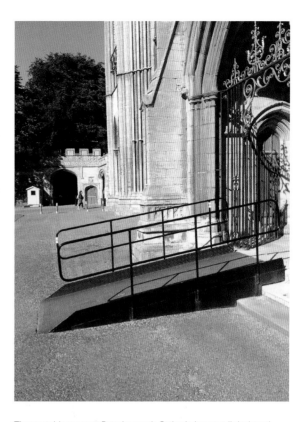

The portable ramp at Peterborough Cathedral was well designed with handrails and a slip-resistant surface. However, it was heavy to move and large to store away; furthermore, it interfered with processional entrances by the choir. The steps that required the ramp have been replaced by a sloping gradient providing step-free access.

usually rely on a detailed knowledge of the building's 'soft spots' and strategic positioning as part of the primary access route on all the floor levels to be connected.

Lift companies offer a wide choice of options to suit budgets, but any final decision should not be based on costs alone. Reliability is vital, both as part of product design but also as part of any contractual agreement in the event of a breakdown. It must always be borne in mind that, in the event of lift failure, a stranded disabled visitor will need to be rescued.

WC Facilities

It would be rare indeed not to find modern plumbing in an historic building, along with electrical and

DAVID BONNETT **ASSOCIATES**
access consultancy research and design

Key

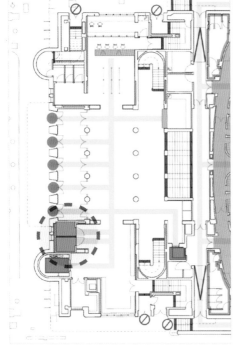

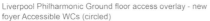

Liverpool Philharmonic Ground floor access overlay - new foyer Accessible WCs (circled)

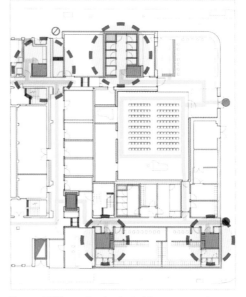

Liverpool Philharmonic extension building access overlay - accessible WCs / change(circled)

In these floor plans the existing WCs services are shown in order to consider the positioning of new accessible WC facilities. Note that the WC locations in blue are distributed in such a way that at least one is adjacent to a lift. All accessible WCs must have lift access available.

communications services. In the past, WC facilities would often be hidden from view and located to the rear of a building. Increasingly, the preference is to have such facilities not only immediately available on arrival, but also to be clearly indicated.

It is usually simpler to connect into existing drainage services than to create new runs. Accessible WCs can often be an adaptation of existing services, but with the requirement for additional manoeuvring space and ideally, they should be located on the principal access route.

With larger, more complicated buildings, it can help to mark on plans all the existing WC locations. An isolated accessible WC will, especially in an entrance foyer, attract the attention of parents with small children, and others. To avoid this, it is preferable to have the accessible WC adjacent to the other main WC facilities. In addition, it is helpful to locate accessible WCs, and even all WCs adjacent to lifts, on all floor levels. This will aid wayfinding considerably.

Special Areas

Special areas are not the service spaces routinely expected by visitors to historic buildings. They are, instead, the special rooms and spaces that visitors have come to see and that make the building

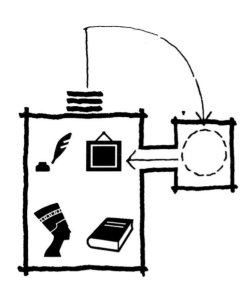

Special areas sketch.

of such interest and possibly unique. Each building will be different in this regard and it is not possible to generalize.

It is with this aspect of inclusive design that the conservation plan becomes a key source of information, designating, as it does, the historic quality of the various parts of the building. Some rooms and spaces within the building and around it will be high on the visitor's to-see list because of their exceptional nature and it may be these very rooms that present the greatest challenge to accessibility.

It is helpful at this point to identify on the plans all such spaces in colour and, in the same manner, to identify the circulation routes to them. This will need to be done for each relevant floor level, ignoring for the moment the absence of lifts unless already installed. By now, an access audit plan will

It is helpful at this point to identify special areas in colour on plans and in the same manner, to identify the circulation routes to them. (Photo: RomanR/Shutterstock.com)

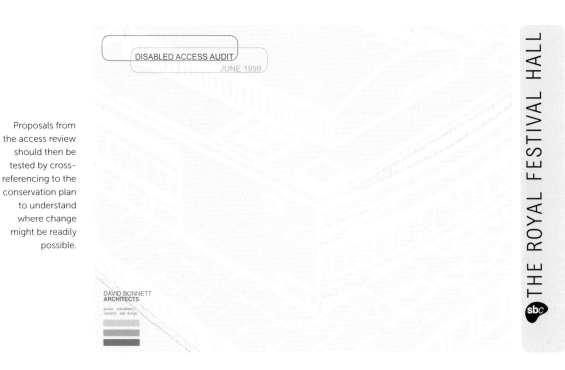

be emerging, identifying what works and what does not. This needs to be tested by cross-referencing any access review proposals with the conservation plan and understanding the scope for change that may or may not be possible. Ultimately, it must rely on the skills of the professionals to explore all possibilities including, where relevant, the introduction of a lift or lifts to the various floor levels.

Escape

The main purpose of any access evaluation is to work out ways of getting disabled people, principally those with limited mobility, into a building. However, it is equally important to then explore how they might get out – escape – in an emergency. This is a complex process that cannot be covered briefly without the risk of oversimplifying, but some helpful ground rules do apply.

Firstly, visitors will be more likely to know intuitively how to get out of a building if it is the same route that they came in. This can often be achieved

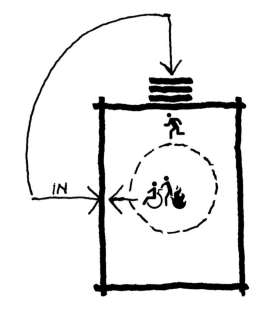

Escape sketch.

in buildings with simple plans on one level, small churches, for example.

Second, complexity increases with building size and with floor levels above and below ground. Where complexity increases, so the need for clarity

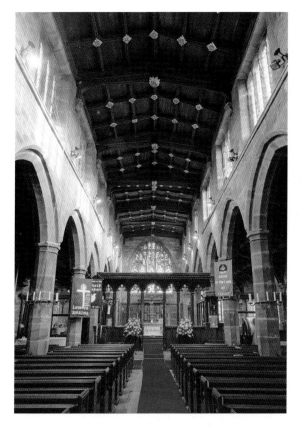

The relatively simple layout of this church provides an intuitive understanding of how the route out is the same as the route in. (Photo: Alastair Wallace/Shutterstock.com)

At Bethnal Green Museum of Childhood, the route out for escape can quite clearly be seen and therefore understood from almost any location.

will increase also. In some cases, the building can assist with this, for example, where clear views enable everyone to see what escape routes are being followed. Conversely, where escape routes are not self-evident, staff must instead be relied on to direct proceedings, especially when there is a reliance on mechanical devices, such as evacuation chairs.

Third, lifts can in some circumstances be used for escape purposes, with this being more likely as the building size increases, especially where the building is divided into Fire Zones. This arrangement can allow visitors dependent on lifts to move out of a danger zone and into an adjoining safe zone and use the lift there.

Chapter Five

Modification

MODIFYING OR REARRANGING AN OBSTA-
cle to physical accessibility will, on a scale
of disruption and physical alteration,
always be an option worth exploring from the outset.
Modifying an existing stepped entrance, for example,
can sometimes be achieved almost imperceptibly.

Overcoming the obstacle may at its simplest and
least disruptive, be achieved by modifying external
ground levels in order to overcome a difference in
levels, or by making a visually discrete alteration to
an otherwise unchanged building frontage. In other
cases a more dramatic modification may be necessary
or even welcome, provided the materials used are
appropriate and the design exceptional. Yet again, some
modifications can be made almost imperceptible owing
to the installation of clever well-designed technology.

The following are all examples of these options and
what they share is the common objective of achieving
step-free accessibility into an historic building with,
at first sight, little evidence of alteration.

Main Case Study: Queens House Greenwich, London

Project Details:	
Sector:	Museum
Location:	London
Completion:	2000
Architects:	Allies and Morrison
Client:	Royal Museums Greenwich

Modification
sketch.

OPPOSITE: Queen's House, Greenwich.

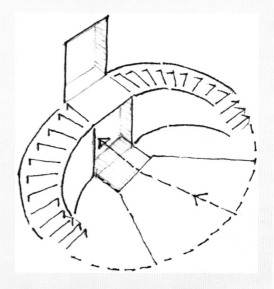

Modification sketch for Queen's House Greenwich.

Historic Background

Queen's House is a former royal residence, built between 1616 and 1635 in Greenwich for Anne of Denmark, the consort of King James I. Its architect was Inigo Jones. Queen's House is recognized as one of the most important buildings in British architectural history, being the first classical building to have been constructed in the country. It was Jones's first major commission after returning from his Grand Tour in Italy. In its day, Jones's Palladian-inspired residence would have appeared revolutionary to English eyes. It was built as an adjunct to the Tudor Palace of Greenwich, a rambling, red-brick building in a vernacular style.

The house's original use was short – seven years – before the English Civil War began in 1642 and swept away the court culture from which it sprang. At the end of the seventeenth century, the Queen's House, though scarcely used, provided the focus for Christopher Wren's Greenwich Hospital. At that time Mary II insisted that the vista to the water from the Queen's House should not be impaired.

Today, the building is both a Grade I listed building and a scheduled ancient monument. It forms part of the National Maritime Museum and is used to display parts of their collection of maritime paintings and portraits.

Built of brick and faced with Portland stone, the Queen's House consists of two storeys. The east and west façades are connected to wings of the house via long colonnades. Internally, the Great Hall is cube-shaped and measures a little over 12m in height, length and width – proportions inspired by Palladio's works. Another Palladio-inspired feature is the Tulip Stair, a continuous balustrade of wrought iron adorned with leaves and tulip flowers. It is the first unsupported helical stairs to be built in England.

Case Study

There are some high profile historic building projects where the experienced architect will steer clear of what appears to be the obvious course of action. This is usually on the assumption that certain 'obvious' features of the building simply cannot be altered.

Such was the case, in the first instance, with the Queen's House in Greenwich. In principle, it

This early photograph of the building shows the famous horseshoe steps up to the main entrance. It also clearly shows the original undercroft doorway, which was approached down three steps. The aim was to modify this arrangement in order to provide a single step-free entrance for everyone.

For many years step-free entry into the Queen's House was at the rear of the building using this ramp. Entry at this point took the wheelchair user into the Great Hall level of the house but to no other levels.

had already been decided that a more appropriate entrance into the building for the visiting public should be via the lower crypt level. This level had the potential to accommodate new visitor facilities needed to prepare the museum for the next decade to come. As the existing crypt entrance was down some steps, alternative options for step-free entry had first to be explored.

For some years, a small ramp at the rear of the building had been relied on for wheelchair-user entry, but it was distinctly a back-door solution. Modifying the famous front 'horseshoe' steps was, of course, deemed inconceivable. Instead, attention focused on providing a discrete ramp or platform lift to a new entrance at the side of the building. This idea was considered only a little better than the back-door solution and for this reason, a combination of client will and architectural expertise provided the necessary determination to tackle the problem head on. A separate side entrance option for wheelchair users was rejected!

With the new side entrance option rejected, the original undercroft entrance was looked at more closely. Its central location beneath the symmetrical steps meant that the doorway was in full view, but – no doubt to reduce its visibility on approach – it was slightly hidden down three steps. Measurements were taken on site and it transpired that there was ample room to eliminate the need for these steps by the creation of a gentle ramp.

The difficulty with this idea was that the ramp would, in turn, necessitate lowering the ground level in front of the unalterable, horseshoe steps. This was what might be described as a catch-22 situation.

This plan shows how the central crypt doorway was originally down several steps. This was the issue to be addressed.

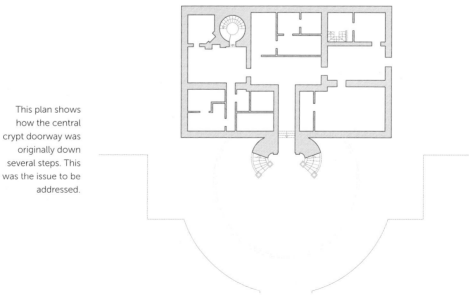

The big idea was to eliminate the steps to the undercroft doorway and to create a ramped approach path down to entrance level. The photograph shows how this was ingeniously achieved by adding two steps to the horseshoe staircase on either side.

The Big Idea

The conundrum of the levels and steps was addressed by the decision to modify the horseshoe steps. This meant excavating down and adding two additional treads. Given the Grade 1 listing of the building, this was an imaginative decision but it required considerable justification. As is often the case, with a combination of expert attention to detailing, selection of the most appropriate materials and firm assurances regarding craftsmanship, it was accepted that this proposal would not only be visually acceptable but also a practical improvement.

A photograph of the staircase entrance showing the original steps down to the undercroft. (Photo: Historic England Archive)

The successful final outcome has been achieved without drawing attention to the change. The staircase plinth has been lowered to accommodate the gentle slope of the new approach path and the path itself is generously wide, thereby avoiding the appearance of a ramp.

Context

The project came into being as part of a wider programme of improvements in anticipation of the Millennium in 2000, with the Royal Observatory site an important location for these celebrations. As part of the programme, the Queen's House would become a Museum of Time, presenting the development of historic timepieces through a specially curated exhibition. This, in turn, would provide a one-off opportunity to upgrade the building to better suit more demanding visitor expectations. These would include space for an information and ticketing desk on arrival and for new cloakrooms. Since the project would, in part, be funded from public resources such as HLF, inclusive design was high on the agenda.

Arrival

The Queen's House is one of several well-known and highly popular buildings that make up the large Royal Museums Greenwich complex, with inevitably long walking distances between each building. Arrival by car is therefore the most practical option for people with restricted mobility, and designated disabled car parking bays are accordingly made available at Devonport House. This facility is mainly intended to serve the National Maritime Museum close by. The onward journey to the Queen's House is a further 100m, necessitating a wheelchair for many.

On the far left is Devonport House where Blue Badge parking is located. It is then necessary to walk the considerable distance from there to the Queen's House itself. The need for this arrangement, though inconvenient for some, is to avoid visitors' cars disturbing the uncluttered view of the house on approach.

It was fortunate that the original doorway was sufficiently wide for wheelchair entry, such that no modifications were required.

involved a major piece of building surgery. In order to create the shaft, the original service staircase had to be carefully dismantled from the undercroft level right the way up through the two floors above. The lift car and an entire new staircase had to be installed within the original stairwell footprint.

Given the space constraints, the lift car could not be designed according to the usual recommended dimensions. It could be greater in width but had to be reduced in depth. The testing of a mock-up reassured the design team that so long as the lift car doors could be made extra wide – and they could – the proposed arrangement, though tight, would work. Similarly, the new staircase was close to recommended design limits, but with careful detailing, it was also made to work.

This highlights a practical difficulty with many historic locations where private vehicles, or even taxis, cannot park directly outside. The reasons will be various and can, in some instances, be overcome by a visitor transport service using electric 'buggies'. Such a service was trialled at Greenwich but found to be incompatible on routes shared with pedestrians.

Building Entry and Foyer

On arrival, there is a single entrance for all visitors using the undercroft doorway, now approached down the gentle slope. This doorway required no modification to its width, which, though modest, is adequate for a wheelchair to pass through. The doorway takes visitors directly into a foyer where the visit can be planned. Given the modest scale of the Queen's House, there are no refreshment facilities, but a cloakroom and toilets are provided, including an accessible WC.

Circulation

Onward circulation for visitors is by lift and stairs. The creation of a shaft for the lift, located in a stairwell,

The replacement staircase was cleverly designed to meet all necessary requirements, but at the same time occupying considerably less space than the original.

The design of the lift was determined by the space available for constructing the lift shaft. This required the lift car to break convention by being wider than it is deep. This, in turn, required a wider doorway than is usual in order to allow entry with a wheelchair.

Fortunately, two further staircases are available for use, including the famous Tulip Stairs.

Emergency Escape

Having managed to deliver visitors to upper levels, the question of how they then might come down again in an emergency will need to be addressed. Since most passenger lifts cannot be used for emergency escape, this will always raise special concerns. In the case of Queen's House, the building is usefully constructed on a banked terrace with three levels on the north side and two on the south at garden level.

This means that direct step-free escape to the outside from both these two levels is possible. For the final third level, a safe refuge is provided, adjoining the designated escape stairs. From here and in the event of an emergency, staff would have to physically assist people unable to use stairs.

The green plan on the left shows how, by eliminating the entrance steps, the entire basement floor is step-free. The new lift and staircase can be seen on the top right hand corner of the plan. The red plan on the right indicates that the whole of the basement floor was originally inaccessible because of the stepped entrance.

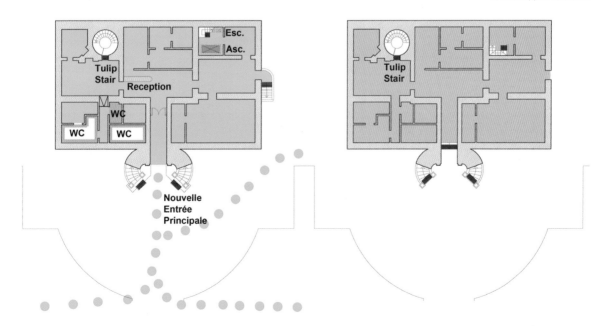

Case Study: Royal Institute of British Architects (RIBA), London

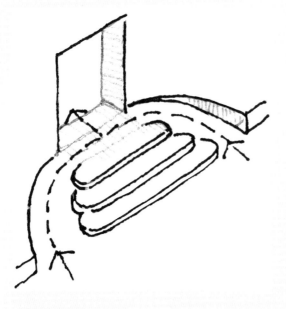

Modification sketch for RIBA.

Project Details:	
Sector:	Commercial
Location:	London
Completion:	1984
Architects:	Douglas Stephen & Partners
Client:	Royal Institute of British Architects

The front entrance to RIBA will be familiar to all architects in the UK and to many around the world. For most, the three shallow front steps from pavement level up to the entrance would barely be noticed on entering. But for a wheelchair user, a visit had only been possible if staff assembled a temporary metal ramp across the steps or physically lifted the visitor in and out.

The entrance steps as they existed before modification. (Photo: Architectural Press Archive/RIBA Collections)

As part of a project to upgrade visitor facilities, the institute wished to meet new expectations for accessibility. The appointed architects were therefore briefed with the challenge of devising a solution to providing step-free access along with other internal changes. Given that the building is Grade II* listed, any external change, especially to the famous entrance, had to be achieved while maintaining the architectural integrity of the building. Different possibilities were considered, but because there is only one visitor entrance to the institute, the entrance steps had to be the focus of change.

The design option taken forward was to modify the existing shallow entrance steps by cutting in symmetrical ramps on either side. The use of stone as a material is unchanged and so too the form and style. The ramp design is deliberately understated and just sufficient in width and gradient for its purpose.

The outcome is not only effective, but also probably goes unnoticed by most visitors. It is fitting that such an excellent example of a modification exists at the entrance

The three steps up to the RIBA entrance have been modified to provide a step-free gradient that is so well executed it looks part of the original design.

to the institute's headquarters in London, sending a clear message to all members of the profession.

Case Study: Kew Palace, London

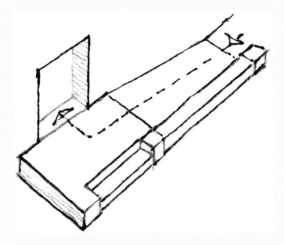

Modification sketch for Kew Palace.

Project Details:

Sector:	Commercial
Location:	London
Completion:	2006
Architects:	Purcell
Client:	Historic Royal Palaces

A similar, though more complicated, modification was undertaken at Kew Palace in 2006 as part of a refurbishment programme. The general aim was to present the story of the occupation of the palace by King George III and his family by the careful restoration of original finishes and materials and the placement of original furniture and fabrics. But an associated aim, since the building would now become a museum, was to ensure that access was possible for all visitors, regardless of disability.

As is so often the case, the first obstacle to step-free access was the front entrance itself, approached by brick steps and unchanged since the building's construction in 1800. Their simple design offered little scope for alteration and the Grade I listed status of the palace would limit any prospect of alteration. However, a solution had to be found, and after considering other options, a key decision was made to carefully dissemble the steps and, by methodically setting aside the original materials, reassemble them in a slightly different position sufficient to be able to form a new front entrance landing.

The original stone entrance steps have been brought forward to provide a landing. This is wide enough for a shallow ramp to one side to be discretely hidden on approach by a low brick plinth wall.

To one side of the landing a short ramp was constructed using carefully selected bricks to match the existing ones. The ramp was designed to be as simple in appearance as possible, just sufficient to achieve its purpose and no more. Critically, any change had to be virtually unnoticeable on approach and for this reason the ramp is discretely screened by a low plinth made of the same bricks as those forming the walls. To further minimize evidence of change, the ramp has no handrail, made acceptable by its short length and shallow rise.

The final outcome is a carefully thought-through compromise between achieving a means of step-free access that adopts a minimalist access solution, but one that is practical in use, allowing this essential part of the project to gain conservation approval and proceed. This is an excellent example of how with a common interest in success a strategy based on the potential for reinstatement at a future date was able to satisfy all those concerned.

Despite the modest scale of Kew Palace, some key internal improvements were possible, but they would only be of benefit if a solution could be found for overcoming the difficulty posed by the original front steps. There was no scope for altering the steep flight of steps at the rear.

Case Study: V&A Museum of Childhood, Bethnal Green, London

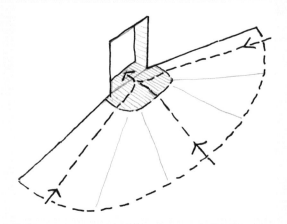

Modification sketch for the V&A Museum of Childhood.

Project Details:	
Sector:	Museum
Location:	London
Completion:	2007
Architects:	Caruso St John Architects
Client:	Victoria & Albert Museum

The Bethnal Green museum was originally the east London branch of the Victoria & Albert Museum and first opened its doors to the public in 1872. A century later, in 1974, it became what is now so fondly known as the Museum of Childhood.

Despite being designated a museum for children, the entrance steps into the museum remained, making few concessions for small children or parents pushing prams. In acknowledgement of this difficulty, a timber ramp was constructed. But despite the practical benefits, its timber construction did little to enhance the appearance of this Grade II listed building.

As part of a major upgrade to the museum in 2005, the client was fully supportive of improving accessibility both into and within the building. Inherent to the process, the architects reviewed options for modifying the front steps or even eliminating them altogether.

After careful investigation of external levels, the latter option was found to be feasible. It was evident

The original steps that for many years were an obstacle to easy access, not least for parents with buggies and prams. For a while a wooden ramp existed but it added nothing of benefit to the character of the building.

that if a line was struck between the pavement level and the internal floor level of the building, a gentle gradient could be achieved without any steps being necessary. This was possible for two reasons: first, the approach area to the building was considerable, allowing a gentle rise over a relatively long distance, and second, the front area surface had no particular architectural merit, thus providing the scope for such a significant but worthwhile modification. Investigation of archive material also made clear that the original forecourt was designed as a slope suitable for visitors to drive in and out by horse and carriage.

When combined, these facts provided a strong case, not only for achieving step-free access but also for making full and better use of the forecourt as a play area.

The new decorative panels enclose a welcome entrance loggia on the same level as the museum interior. The original steps have been made redundant by gently sloping the new forecourt surface toward the doorway. (Photo: Peter St John/Caruso St John Architects)

Case Study: Peterborough Cathedral, Peterborough

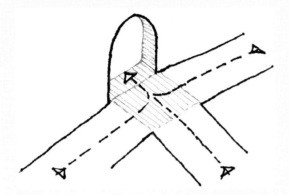

Modification sketch for Peterborough Cathedral.

Project Details:	
Sector:	Place of Worship
Location:	Peterborough
Completion:	2015
Architects:	Whitworth
Client:	Peterborough Cathedral

Like many ancient churches in the UK, Peterborough Cathedral has a grand stone façade approached across a large quadrangle. The entrance to the cathedral, as would be expected, was stepped, restricting access for some and inconveniencing others. The cathedral authorities wished to address this limitation as part of a general improvements project. However, introducing physical changes to the historic frontage of a cathedral requires careful consideration. In many such cases, entrances to the side or rear of the building have been introduced as an alternative. In this case, the cathedral authorities had a clear wish to explore a step-free solution to the front elevation itself.

The first consideration in such circumstances is to consider modifying what already exists, in this case a wide entrance with three shallow stone steps. Given the generous approach area and the existing network of paths, it was evident

Portable ramps can be helpful as a temporary measure, but are rarely suitable as a permanent solution.

that modifying the approach path gradient could obviate the need for steps completely.

Given the large scale of the building, the construction of a short approach ramp might have been an option, but so too was to gradually raise the path level almost imperceptibly over a longer distance. This has allowed the steps to be eliminated altogether and provide, for the first time, step-free access into the cathedral entrance for all.

The generous quadrangle in front of the cathedral has allowed the approach path to be gently raised, removing any need for the original entrance steps. (Photo: Electric Egg Ltd/Adobe Stock)

Case Study: The Treasury – St James's Entrance, London

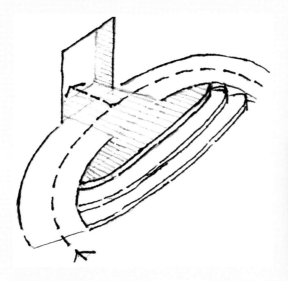

Modification sketch for the Treasury.

Project Details:	
Sector:	Government
Location:	London
Completion:	2002
Architects:	Foster+Partners
Client:	HM Treasury Exchequer Partnership

Despite its importance, the original entrance onto Horse Guards was not only understated it was also difficult for many to use and impossible for some.

HM's Treasury in Whitehall London was subject to a major upgrade in 1996 by Foster & Partners Architects. Part of the design brief was to ensure that anyone, regardless of disability, should be able to work there. As it is a listed building, this presented a range of challenges both externally, getting into the main entrances, and internally.

One such challenge was the entrance from St James's Park where an inset entrance with steps needed to be overcome. Fortunately, the wide pavement in front of the building was available as part of any solution, though insufficient to eliminate the steps as at Peterborough Cathedral or the Museum of Childhood.

In this case, the considerable width of the building frontage suggested that an entrance ramp might be possible. In order to take forward this idea it would be necessary, as at Kew Palace, to dismantle the original steps, but in this instance, replace them with new ones. The steps would be brought sufficiently forward from the building frontage to construct a landing as the arrival point for the ramp.

The question, then, was what form would the ramp take? With classical buildings of the period and scale of the Treasury, symmetry was an inherent part of the design. To introduce a conventional one-sided ramp to the building elevation would jar aesthetically and would not be acceptable, nor would the introduction of highly visible handrails. To address both concerns, a symmetrical ramp design was developed whereby two ramps could be formed, one on either of the landing.

This, is turn, allowed the other concern about highly visible handrails to be addressed. The purpose of the handrails is to provide support when walking up the ramp, with the usual expectation of a rail to both sides as users may be weaker on one side than the other. However, the visual impact of this could be overwhelming, but because there would be two symmetrical ramps, handrails to one side only would be possible in achieving the same benefit but, critically, would substantially reduce the visual impact.

The need for a second flight of internal steps to this entrance was addressed by the insertion of a lift.

The modification to the Horse Guards Treasury entrance is significant and the materials and design are excellent. The symmetrical design allows a single handrail on either side rather than the conventional two handrails that would be needed if there was only one ramp.

Chapter Six

Addition/Extension

THIS TYPOLOGY REFERS TO THE CONSTRUC-tion of a new extension or addition along-side the historic building or sometimes the acquisition of an existing adjoining property. Rather than altering the historic building by adding a level entrance, lifts, cafés and shops, these are, instead, pro-vided within a new or neighbouring structure. This, in turn, connects the new to the old, either directly through existing or new openings or sometimes via a covered way.

In the following five case studies, three are exam-ples of wholly new additions and the remaining two are where the adjoining property has been acquired and been brought into new use as an extension.

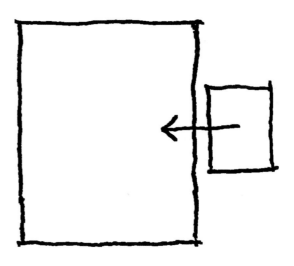

Addition/Extension sketch.

Main Case Study: The Roundhouse, London

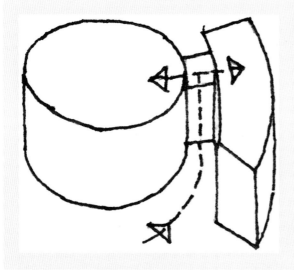

Project Details:	
Sector:	Culture
Location:	London
Completion:	2006
Architects:	John McAslan + Partners
Client:	Norman Trust

Addition/Extension sketch for the Roundhouse.

OPPOSITE: The Roundhouse in North London.

Historic Background

The Camden Roundhouse, known to many in the 1960s and 1970s as the venue for rock concerts or avant-garde theatre, was built in the early days of rail travel as a shed for servicing locomotives. London and North Western Railway engines were driven onto a turntable at the upper level, allowing clinker to be dropped into the vaults below. The turntable could be rotated to allow the correct engine to exit from the shed when required. The clinker deposited into the brick vaults at street level was collected by horse and cart and removed to the outskirts of London.

The circular brick shed, designed by Robert B. Dockray, had a conical slate roof with a ring of glazed roof lights and smoke louvres at its pitch. This roof was supported by twenty-four cast iron Doric columns. In little more than ten years, the shed was rendered redundant as the size of engines increased. The building was then leased as a store for Gilbey's Gin until it was converted into an entertainment venue in the 1960s. As a notable example of mid-nineteenth-century railway architecture, the shed was listed as Grade ll* in 1954.

The building fell into disrepair in the 1970s and was eventually taken over by Camden Council who sold it to the Norman Trust in the 1990s. The Roundhouse Trust was set up and John McAslan and Partners were appointed to prepare designs for a venue that would host world-leading music events, as well as converting the brick vaults into workshops for local young people to learn about the technicalities of the music business.

Working closely with English Heritage (now Historic England), the architects developed a programme of works to repair the historic fabric; transform the central space – with its structure of Doric columns – into a modern, flexible auditorium; create the workshops below for local youngsters; and add a wraparound extension to house the box office, bar and café, art gallery foyer and offices. It is this extension, entered at street level, that holds the key to providing an accessible building. The front of the building has been sensitively landscaped, while step-free glazed doorways to the circular shed allow by-passers to enjoy glimpses of the brickwork vaults.

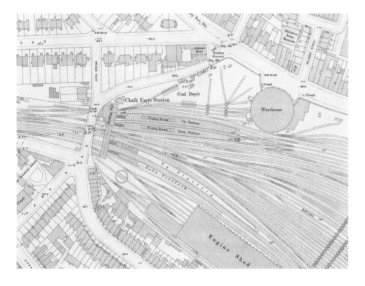

The original function of the Roundhouse as a locomotive turntable was short lived and for several decades it became a storage warehouse for Gilbey's Gin. The building was listed Grade II* in 1954 and shortly afterwards began its new career as an entertainment venue. (Image: Ordnance Survey, London VII.11 Revised: 1894, Published: 1895)

Case Study

A good example of the addition typology is the Roundhouse project in north London. The original function of the building was short-lived and after some decades of industrial and warehouse use, it became, in the 1960s, an arts and cultural venue.

So successfully did it accommodate this new role that in 2004 a decision was made to completely upgrade the building both physically and technically to meet new standards, including improved accessibility. The client envisioned a building serving the community with recording studios, practice rooms and meeting spaces for use during the day, and in the evenings becoming an entertainment venue. An early commitment was for the building and all its facilities to be of special benefit to younger people and to be accessible for all. Since the building was listed Grade II*, the brief somehow had to reconcile these considerable ambitions with the demands for conservation.

A major consideration was the sheer volume of visitors at peak periods buying tickets, needing refreshments, cloakrooms and other facilities. How could the special demands of these provisions be introduced into a round structure defying such a major intervention? It quickly became evident that an alternative design approach would be required. Fortunately, the availability of some adjoining land suggested that a wholly new structure – a new addition – would be possible. With this key understanding in place, the project was able to move forward and the concept developed further.

The form that emerged was a quadrant structure on three floors connected to the Roundhouse itself by a continuous, full-height glazed atrium. Within the new addition would be housed all back-of-house functions and also visitor facilities, including a café, meeting rooms, cloaks and WCs. The atrium would provide a welcoming and spacious entrance foyer lit from above by a glazed roof. Critically for

accessibility, the connecting atrium would provide not only a circulation staircase but also a passenger lift up to the new audience levels.

Arrival

The Roundhouse is positioned in a relatively narrow site bounded to the south by the rail network it once served and to the north by a busy main road. The locality is a dense mix of late Victorian terraced housing sharing space with a wide variety of commercial activities.

On-street parking is at a premium, with visitors having to rely on public transport. This includes buses and a nearby tube station, but while all London buses are accessible, most tube stations are not, the local Chalk Farm station being an example. For disabled visitors to the Roundhouse, buses or taxis are therefore the only real option. Fortunately, the building has a large service yard that, as part of the project, was designed to include space for designated disabled car parking bays. Use of these can be prearranged, with entry via the stage door and on into the lift lobby.

The bays make valuable use of this service yard that is now primarily intended for the considerable

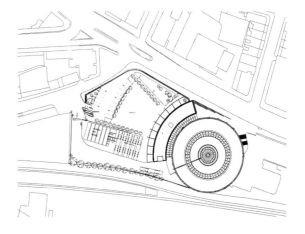

This photo shows the vibrant new extension with café, meeting areas and offices on display. These are linked to the original building on the left by a full height glazed atrium. Note the step-free street level entrance formed in the original wall.

This location plan shows how the site is squeezed between a main road to the north and the railway line to the south. Fortunately, the site included additional land to the west, which is now a car park for the venue. The site also provided space for the construction of the new extension.

traffic generated by visiting rock bands with all their equipment. Disabled visitors using this route might be lucky enough to bump into a rock star.

Building Entry

The front entrance of the Roundhouse faces the main road, opening almost directly onto the sloping public highway. Within the tight strip of building frontage available it was necessary to construct broad steps down from pavement level to the entrance level. Fortunately, since there is little space for a ramp, the slope of the hill does at a convenient point align with the entrance level, allowing step-free access. The final outcome is not perfect, but it does work and is sensibly close to the nearby bus stop.

On entering through the modest doorway, one is amazed by the cleverness of the new architecture as it

unfolds dramatically, directing the visitor around the building curve to the full-height, top-lit atrium. This is an exciting, vibrant place to meet up with friends.

The Facilities

All that the visitor requires is contained within the atrium – ticket desk, cloak rooms, access to the café and, of course, the generous new staircase and new lift to upper and lower levels. All these facilities are in the new addition, barely intruding into the original Roundhouse structure, with the added benefit of few constraints to the choice of colours and materials that might otherwise have applied in a Grade II* listed building.

Additional facilities are installed in the original arched vaults below, which once supported the train shed turntable. These spaces are largely converted into sound studios substantially out of earshot of neighbours.

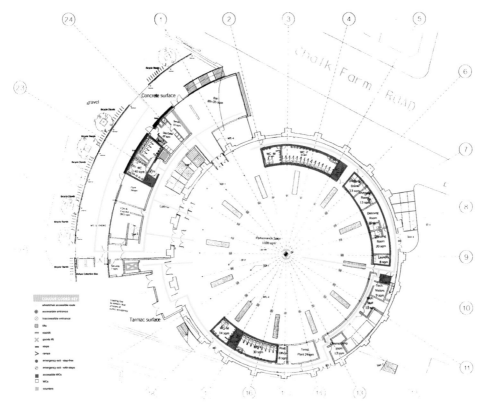

The extension on the left follows the curve of the original building. Connection between new to old was achieved by constructing a full-height glazed atrium accommodating all circulation, stairs and lifts.

ROUNDHOUSE - *Level 1 Plan*

The introduction of daylight in the atrium, where the new construction meets the old, is a helpful device for wayfinding. It is such a key feature in the building design that it is an ideal location for arranging to meet friends on arrival at the theatre – you cannot miss it!

Indeed, a key feature of the main concert hall has been to insulate the building against sound transfer.

Circulation

Movement within the old building is, unsurprisingly, determined by its predominantly round shape. This helps simplify wayfinding and an added touch is the introduction of bright colours on the 'circuit' to help locate where you are.

The original iron frame was retained and a new concert hall structure formed within it, with seating accessed from perimeter circulation routes following the original brick Roundhouse walls. Beneath the original turntable, the supporting radial structure built up as brick vaults is now used as recording studios, music rooms and meeting spaces. While some of the vaults are narrow, some are sufficiently wide for wheelchair circulation.

The Roundhouse design works well for accessibility, providing excellent visitor facilities without disturbing the form of the original building. It has deservedly won many awards over time and with its popularity increasing, a strong case might now be made for not just one passenger lift but for two.

This photo shows the day-lit glazed atrium following the curve of the original building. Within the atrium is the new staircase and to the right, the new lift. The atrium is a successful meeting area linking the new addition with the old building.

Case Study: Kew Palace, London

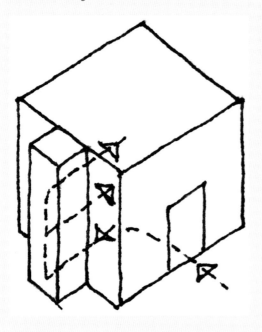

Addition/Extension sketch for Kew Palace.

Project Details:	
Sector:	Historic
Location:	London
Completion:	2006
Architects:	Purcell
Client:	Historic Royal Palaces

The royal palace in Kew Gardens, alongside the river Thames, remained substantially unchanged for two centuries, with its interior waiting to tell the story of its celebrated residents, George III and his family. In the late 1990s, the custodians of the palace, Historic Royal Palaces, embarked on a ten-year restoration programme with the aim of telling this story within the palace rooms themselves. A commitment at the outset was for the restored palace to be accessible to all, including school parties. Quite how this ambition would be fully met was at that time unclear.

The obvious barriers to accessibility to be addressed were how to create step-free entry into the building and then how to move between floor levels inside by lift. The modest residential scale of the palace offered little scope for any internal intervention like a lift shaft, no matter how discrete; instead, it was clear that some form of external addition would need to be devised.

Investigation of early drawings inspired a novel idea. From the plans it was evident that on the west flank of the building once stood a shaft housing water closets on each upper level. The shaft originally connected into the building on each floor at the junction with the servants' staircase. If a new external shaft could be added and the old openings reinstated, it would allow the installation of a lift, with entry on each level. This design concept was approved for further investigation and a feasibility study commenced.

Much thought went into the appearance of the new shaft for it to meet concerns for architectural

This photo shows the staircase wall with original landing connections to the 'privy' clearly evident. Access down to the basement area is now by platform lift and steps in order for it to provide an independent education room facility.

integrity. This led to an unapologetically modern design, scaled down for minimum visual impact. Much thought also went into the internal details to ensure that the tight circulation routes and original closet openings would enable a wheelchair user to enter and exit the lift on each level. With careful detailing, including the chamfering of original brick reveals, accessibility was shown to be possible.

To bring this design concept to fulfilment was a tremendous achievement and so worthwhile, given that step-free circulation on all floors was already practicable once inside. However, this success had to be matched by a solution to the front entrance steps; a challenge that would require similar ingenuity and is covered in Chapter 5. An accepted constraint was that the view of the palace on approach should appear unaltered. For the lift extension, a similar constraint applied. This was possible as the new lift shaft was sufficiently far back on the west façade that it would be out of view. As always in these situations, careful detailing and choice of materials were key, along with a degree of flexibility in the lift landing designs. These modest compromises were judged wholly acceptable in the circumstances.

Opened in 2006 to celebrate the Queen's eightieth birthday, the project has been a great success, providing, as it does, full accessibility. In the wider ambition to make the narrative equally accessible, technology has been relied on. Images are projected on to the walls of family rooms retelling the stories of the royal residents. Information wands and earphones enable those who cannot see to engage in the experience, along with the audible magic of being in an old palace, with original creaking floorboards and all.

The new externally positioned lift shaft, built of modern materials, is positioned to connect it with the original staircase landings inside. Its minimal 'footprint' avoids it being evident when the palace is approached from the front.

Case Study: Whitechapel Art Gallery, London

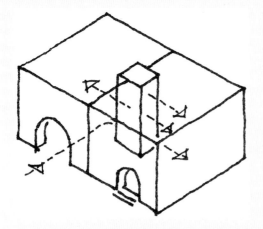

Addition/Extension sketch for Whitechapel.

Project Details:	
Sector:	Gallery
Location:	London
Completion:	2009
Architects:	Witherford Watson Man
Client:	Trustees of the Whitechapel Gallery

The Whitechapel Art Gallery opened in 1901 and was the first purpose-built publicly funded art gallery in London at that time. The building is locked into its position on a busy commercial road, with a public library on one side that incorporates the entrance to a tube station. Internal alterations to the original gallery had been made in 1986 in an effort to expand capacity and add supporting facilities such as a café upstairs and an entrance level shop. But, inevitably, a limit to expansion was reached and the access improvements made were, in keeping with that time, limited.

When in 2008 the neighbouring public library was vacated and became available, the opportunity for a long-overdue expansion was seized. Having acquired its neighbour, the gallery needed to consider how this opportunity could best be exploited, including how it could achieve a comprehensive inclusive design. This was a stated commitment at the outset by the client and fully supported by public funding.

The distinctive gallery entrance on the left was made step-free in 1986 by re-forming the original steps into a gentle slope. The stepped library entrance on the right remains unchanged. (Photo: GrindtXX, CC BY-SA 4.0 via Wikimedia Commons)

As part of the initial feasibility study, an audit of the existing gallery identified step-free circulation between floor levels as a major weakness. Despite detailed efforts to improve the original gallery staircase, it remained difficult for many to use, and those requiring a lift had to use the original service lift with cage doors. As staff had to operate the lift, this involved waiting time for the visitor.

Using the library building to address these shortcomings was therefore an important part of the brief. In effect, the 'next door' building was seen as an addition that could accommodate the expanded café and restaurant areas, treble the gallery space and provide additional meeting rooms. However, this would not be a simple matter since floor levels between the two buildings did not align, other than at entry level.

These problems were resolved in two ways. First, the library staircase was retained as the main means of vertical circulation in the old library and for the rest of the gallery. With its conventional design providing handrails and half landings, it was substantially suitable for this purpose, even by current standards. Second, the centrepiece of the access improvements would be the construction of a wholly new passenger lift. This would be at the junction of the two buildings, adjacent to the original dividing party wall, and would provide access to all levels in both buildings. The installation has worked well, though it can still mean a degree of extended waiting time for the lift at peak periods. But the installation has proved reliable over time. The original lift

remains available for back-of-house functions and critically, it provides a means of back-up in case of lift failure.

The availability of the library building unlocked huge potential that will serve the gallery for many years to come. Using it as an addition to the gallery has proved wholly justified. The new arrangement works well, supported by the careful positioning of directional signage to the various facilities.

The all-important new opening through the party wall at entrance level connects the two adjoining buildings. Critically, it also provides access to the new lift serving all upper levels. Beyond is the retained library staircase.

Case Study: The Garden Museum, London

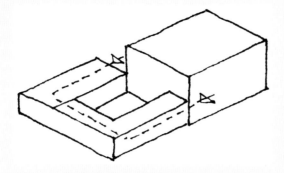

Addition/Extension sketch for the Garden Museum.

Project Details:	
Sector:	Museum
Location:	London
Completion:	2017
Architects:	Dow Jones Architects
Client:	The Garden Museum

The Garden Museum next to Lambeth Palace in London is a clever variation on the theme of addition/extension. The museum came into being five years after the Church of St Mary-at-Lambeth ceased to serve its dwindling congregation of parishioners in 1972. The church premises included a small churchyard, the final resting place of several eminent people, including plant hunter and gardener John Tradescant and William Bligh, the famous captain of HMS *Bounty*. The church took on its new role as a museum in 1977.

Following its early years of success, a major upgrade took place in 2008, making full use of the original church building, including the ingenious construction of an upper-level gallery for additional exhibition space. In addition to a new staircase, a small lift was also installed, demonstrating the early commitment to ensuring that the museum

Captain Bligh's tomb can be seen in the old churchyard with other gravestones commemorating notable historic figures.

would be fully accessible. Despite the success of this upgrade, the museum decided in 2015 to raise public funds for a new project to consider how the exhibition space might be increased even further and how additional income could be earned beyond the regular membership subscriptions and earnings from the café and shop. A proposal was developed for the doubling of exhibition space, the addition of new meeting rooms, event spaces and classrooms, and for the creation of a fully staffed restaurant with its own kitchen and food store to enable the museum to earn income.

To accommodate these ambitious proposals would not be possible in the fully occupied church building, so the extension/addition option was the only one that was feasible. This might have been achieved by adding an adjoining building, but not at the risk of clearing the churchyard. Given its celebrated 'residents' and the listed status of their tombs, any such option was unlikely to be approved. Instead, the architect designed a new extension comprised of connected rooms, but critically, all built around the churchyard, preserving

the wonderful graves and headstones. This solution has created an internal courtyard enclosed by the new rooms, now a perfectly sheltered open space ideal for nurturing exotic and unusual plants. Each of the new rooms – the restaurant, meeting rooms and event spaces – has a view directly onto the courtyard, so there are no concerns about being overlooked. The room windows are fully glazed, with some opening directly onto an open ambulatory.

With the entire new addition at ground level, the circulation routes are step-free, providing easy access to all the facilities, including new WCs. One side of the courtyard cleverly connects with the church wall and its existing doorway without disturbing the original fabric. As a further practical benefit, the restaurant can be approached either direct from the street, as in the evenings, or via the church building during museum opening times. The project has deservedly received many design awards and is an instructive example of how to make best use of a new extension for ensuring comprehensive accessibility.

Bligh's tomb is now the centrepiece of the enclosed courtyard garden looked onto from the new restaurant and meeting rooms. To the right is the ambulatory connecting the church building with the new facilities.

The glazed ambulatory successfully provides a link between the original church building on the left and the new courtyard enclosure on the right.

Case Study: Royal Academy of Arts, London

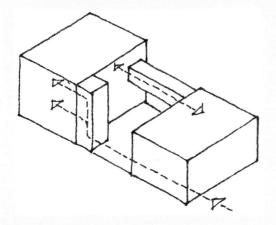

Addition/Extension sketch for the Royal Academy of Art.

Project Details:	
Sector:	Commercial
Location:	London
Completion:	2018
Architects:	David Chipperfield Architects
Client:	Royal Academy of Arts

First created in 1768 with the support of George III, the Royal Academy of Arts (RAA) moved a hundred years later into its current premises, Burlington House off Piccadilly. Like all successful institutions, the academy continued over time to increase its membership and activities, looking always for scope to expand.

To its rear, No. 6 Burlington Gardens was constructed around the same time, originally as part of University College London, and much later when it became the Museum of Mankind. In 1997 the museum relocated elsewhere, leaving No. 6 vacant. For the RAA, this represented a unique opportunity for expansion into its neighbouring building and negotiations for acquisition commenced. Feasibility studies for physically linking the two buildings began two decades later.

The RAA had already made efforts to improve access to its Piccadilly building prompted by the expectations of the Disability Discrimination Act 1995. The most obvious difficulty at that time was the grand raised portico entrance from the Addenburg Courtyard up into the museum building. A holding measure was put in place by the construction of a timber ramp that did little justice to the building. When HLF funding for the project became available, the old ramp was replaced with an elegant new ramp in stone. Similarly, the raised portico entrance to No. 6 Burlington Gardens was also cleverly modified to provide step-free access.

However, the real challenge to the architect was how to successfully link Burlington House with Burlington Gardens in order to provide comprehensive

The original vaulted corridor was previously a busy service area with mechanical and electrical conduits and pipes that had accumulated over the years.

accessibility across the expanded RAA site. Any solution would be far from simple since the link would have to cross an open service yard below, across Lovelace Courtyard and separately across the Vaults, all of which had to remain in operation.

Given the considerable difference in levels between the two buildings, initial thoughts of a ramped solution were soon rejected. Ramps are, of course, reliable and functional, but beyond a certain height difference, the effort required to physically manage the ramp becomes counter-productive and unacceptable.

Instead, two separate solutions were devised to cross the divide. The difference in levels across the Lovelace Courtyard was such that an enclosed sloping bridge could be constructed. This is a pleasant experience for all to use and provides tempting views of the courtyard gardens below. By contrast, the difference on either side across the Vaults is considerable, more than a gentle gradient could overcome. In this case, a spectacular staircase makes the connection but with its height clearly beyond the capability of some visitors. To ensure access for all, two adjoining passenger lifts have been installed to supplement the staircase.

The project was a major undertaking, involving considerable fundraising to make the very best use of the opportunities that the neighbouring acquisition provided. This combination of a bridge link, a new staircase and two new lifts has been necessary to provide the comprehensive accessibility that was confidently expected by the client, the funders and RAA members themselves.

The bridge crossing over Lovelace Courtyard, its large window providing views into the courtyard below. Levels across the courtyard were such that only a gentle slope for the bridge was required.

This elegant vaulted corridor now links both buildings at lower level. At the far end can be seen one of the new staircases, to the right of which are two new lifts.

Chapter Seven

Insertion

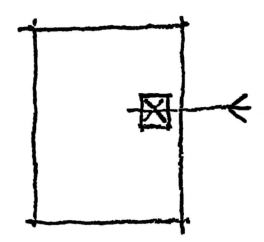

Insertion sketch.

Main Case Study: Royal Festival Hall, London

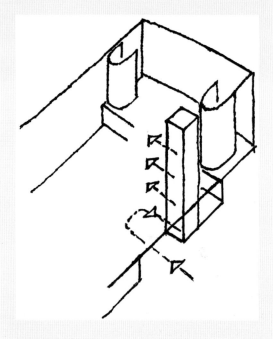

Insertion sketch for the Royal Festival Hall.

A S THE NAME SUGGESTS, THIS TERM IMPLIES identifying a location within an historic building where a lift might be inserted in order to provide step-free access between floor levels. The 'insertion' may be part of a wider range of changes, but once the location of the lift has been agreed in principle, most other access considerations fall into place.

In this chapter there are five case studies, all listed buildings. Three cover the insertion of a wholly new lift providing step-free access between levels for the first time in each building's history. These buildings have in common relatively low levels of lift use; in two cases the lift is operated by a member of staff. The other two studies are examples of providing a new lift in addition to an existing one, which is too remote or simply insufficient to adequately serve a major building upgrade. These buildings have a high level of use and the lifts are entirely operated by visitors themselves.

OPPOSITE: The Royal Festival Hall from Hungerford Bridge.

Project Details:	
Sector:	Culture
Location:	London
Completion:	2008
Architects:	Allies and Morrison
Client:	Southbank Centre

This shows the original service road at riverside level providing entry into the building for disabled visitors, including informal car parking. This arrangement ceased with the 2005 upgrade that required a solution to compensate for its loss. (Photo: Architectural Press Archive/RIBA Collections)

Historic Background

Opened for the Festival of Britain in 1951, the Royal Festival Hall (RFH) is a much loved Grade l listed building on London's South Bank. The pedestrian route it created along the south bank of the river significantly increased in prominence in the years that followed. By the early 1960s expectations from national and international audiences generated proposals for a comprehensive renewal project to provide enhanced acoustics in the concert hall and upgraded facilities throughout the building.

As a result, the RFH was reoriented in 1964, with the addition of foyers, terraces and improved entranceways on to the riverside. These changes have, in turn, been affected, both positively and negatively, by the construction of raised walkways to serve the neighbouring Queen Elizabeth Hall, Purcell Room and Hayward Gallery, all built in the late 1960s. In the 1970s and 1980s the construction of the National Theatre and National Film Theatre and the opening of the Globe, all contributed to yet further enjoyment of a riverside stroll. Today, following the construction of the Millennium Footbridge linking St Paul's with Tate Modern, it is estimated that 70 per cent of visitors to London walk along the South Bank at some point during their stay.

The 1964 Addition

The purpose of the 1964 addition was to provide large riverside foyers each connected to concert hall foyers by grand staircases and lifts. The foyers were a welcome addition and are still much valued, both as generous meeting spaces and for their unrestricted views across the river Thames towards Westminster and the City of London.

However, at the time of designing in 1964, it was not felt necessary to connect the new foyers directly to upper concert hall levels by lifts.

The 2005 Upgrade

Interest in improving accessibility at the RFH arose in part from the Disability Discrimination Act, along with the desire by the South Bank Centre to increase visitor numbers, a desire that was given impetus by the construction of new pedestrian bridges linking the South Bank to both Charing Cross and the City on the north side of the river. The head of visitor services recognized the potential benefits of these new routes across the river for increasing visitor numbers and was determined that improved accessibility would

The pedestrian route in the photograph was an addition to the railway bridge in 2005. It was successful in bringing a large number of visitors from Westminster on the north side of the river to the Festival Hall complex on the south. Notably, the new bridge connection included public lifts at either end.

feature as part of the upgrade. This was an early example of accessible urban design being applied to a busy part of London's public realm.

An important rationale for change to the building itself came as a result of working closely with the conservation architect and developing an understanding of the building's original plan. This had originally promoted entry on each side of the building, rather than from the riverside, with the aim of welcoming visitors into the generous spaces beneath the auditorium. By restoring the primacy of these original approaches it would be possible to achieve comprehensive step-free access to the RFH by the creation of two new lifts at key points. The upstream lift would be external and take visitors from street level up to the riverside level and the downstream lift would be internal, taking visitors again from street level and, for the first time, to all concert hall levels.

Consultation

At the outset of the project and at the behest of the HLF, the RFH formed a consultation access group

Completing a comprehensive network of accessible step-free pedestrian routes required a new lift from street level to the upper riverside terrace. The new lift can be seen here (in yellow) and was installed as part of the upgrade project. The lift is managed by the Southbank Centre for public use.

The new internal passenger lift completed the network of accessible routes. Given its anticipated use, it is not only large but designed to be easily seen. It is celebrated by having a fully glazed lift shaft and conveys visitors from street level to all concert hall levels above.

to help identify potential access improvements. In this way a comprehensive access audit, coupled with access group comments, helped formulate the case for change and achieve funding from ACE and listed building consent from the local authority.

Inserting the Lift

To arrive at a well-informed decision on the location of new lifts, it was important that the preferred points of arrival by disabled visitors should be fully understood. The access group played an important role in this process. Their view was that the downstream entrance was without question the preferred location. It would provide an internal connection from street level to all other levels without the need for steps. Furthermore, it was on this side that new Blue Badge car parking was proposed, under the control of the RFH itself. The logic was clear and it then remained for the exact structural position for the lift shaft to be agreed.

To cut lift shaft openings into reinforced concrete slabs on all levels required expert assessment by structural engineers. This is particularly the case with twentieth-century buildings when compared to more traditional timber joist construction. Regarding the lift car design, it was anticipated that at peak

periods the 'new' lift would be busy and that the passenger load could be expected to include several wheelchair users at any one time. To avoid extended waiting times and queues, the lift car was designed to be extra large and to effectively announce its visual presence the lift is enclosed in a glass shaft so that it can clearly be seen 'on the move'.

The original staircases from the riverside foyer level still function perfectly well and remain unchanged. They are, of course, now supplemented by the new lift.

Other Improvements

Another original feature of the RFH was the positioning of WC facilities for men and women on opposite sides of the building. To help find these, wayfinding was assisted by the use of the colours red and green to identify the port and starboard sides of the building. Whether or not these nautical references really helped is another question, but the convention of 'gender' separation in this way no longer finds favour. It was not much appreciated by the access group either, who were far more interested in the introduction of accessible WCs distributed in sensible locations on all levels. This meant that they should be reached in a reasonably quick time, not least during the all-too-short concert intervals.

Seating

Providing access for wheelchair users to all concert hall levels meant that new space had to be found to accommodate them. Considerable success was achieved on this point, with thirty-two spaces provided with a wide range of 'seating' options. But, of course, many members of the audience, though not in wheelchairs, experience limited mobility inhibiting their use of stairs, especially the steep steps associated with audience seating. To address this, some aisles on entry to the stalls, circle and balcony levels were provided with 'easy access seating', that is seats with slightly increased leg room and up or down no more than two steps.

Artists and Musicians

It is easy to consider the needs of disabled audience members to the exclusion of performers who may also have special needs. The access group was keen to ensure that some at least of the new changing rooms should be made fully accessible – they were – and critically, step-free access provided to both the stage and the orchestra pit. The moving of large instruments like pianos on and off stage was a routine activity for stage staff using mechanical lifts, so an adapted version of this approach was adopted.

Escape

Finally, the key test of all such ambitions is not just getting mobility-impaired people into a building but also getting them out in the event of an emergency. At the time of the project and even now, it is the convention for mobility-impaired people to wait until others have first left the auditorium via the fire stairs. Only then are slow-movers directed by support staff to 'safe areas', from where assisted escape can commence.

The great achievement of the 2005 upgrade was to succeed in providing step-free access to all concert hall levels, including the boxes on either side of the auditorium. In addition, spaces were created for wheelchair users in front of the stalls and at the half level on the left. (Photo: Allies and Morrison)

Case Study: Sir John Soane's Museum, London

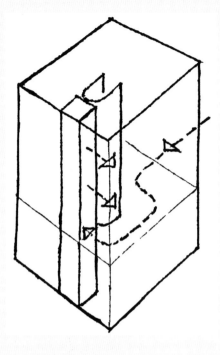

Insertion sketch for Soane Museum.

The original stone staircase has survived regular use remarkably well. To the rear of the stairwell on each level was a closet, each directly above the other. The well now serves as the lift shaft.

Project Details:	
Sector:	Museum
Location:	London
Completion:	2009
Architects:	Julian Harrap Architects
Client:	The Trustees of Sir John Soane's Museum

The outstanding features of the Soane Museum, once home to the architect Sir John Soane, are its originality and the fact that it has remained substantially unchanged for 200 years. Its display of architectural models and drawings, sculpture and artefacts is arranged with dramatic effect on several floors. These gallery spaces link directly to what were once family rooms, a library and drawing office. Soane wished the museum to be open to all for educational purposes, though since its opening in 1837 only those able to climb stairs could benefit.

In 1997 the new Director proposed that this limitation should be addressed as part of a wider scheme for acquiring the property next door and opening more of the private rooms to visitors. This ambition raised the inevitable question of 'how'? The buildings, since there are three connected together, are all Grade I listed, severely restricting any scope for physical alteration. How could a lift, for example, be installed for step-free access between levels if indeed this was possible at all?

The feasibility study began with a detailed access audit of the building and a review of measured plans. These revealed that to the rear of the main staircase in No. 14 was, on each level, a closet, each stacked neatly above the other. The closets had for some years been stripped of their original fittings and used for storage. Each of these rooms were accessed from an adjoining larger room via a doorway. It became clear that it might be possible to install a lift shaft within the stack, but to be acceptable to trustees and conservationists, the whole installation would need to be 'invisible'.

To install a lift shaft within such tight constraints required a bespoke solution and also some flexibility regarding the minimum space dimensions that usually apply. This was made acceptable by the decision to rely on the use of a special narrow wheelchair of the type used in aircraft. Visitors would need to transfer into this special chair in order to manoeuvre through the narrow galleries as well as to use the lift. In addition, the visitor would enjoy the benefit of being conducted on the tour by a well-informed, well-trained member of staff. With these provisos accepted, the design could proceed.

In order to test the installation, there were practice runs on site before opening to visitors in wheelchairs. This was a vital component in ensuring success. As to being 'invisible', this required both the lift and lift lobbies to be contained within the closet footprint, out of view. To achieve this, the lobby door from the library is hidden behind a secret door 'masquerading' as part of the library bookshelves.

The successful insertion of this lift in a Grade I listed building reflects the resolve of all those concerned to achieve what seemed at first to be impossible.

The small passenger lift is entered at ground floor level via the Library Room. The lift lobby door is disguised by a false bookcase front. The lift is operated by a trained visitor escort. (©Dennis Gilbert/VIEW)

Case Study: Hackney Empire Theatre, London

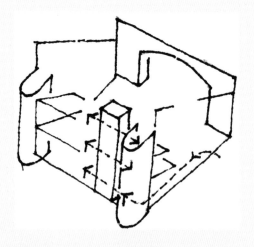

Insertion sketch for the Hackney Empire.

Project Details:	
Sector:	Theatre
Location:	London
Completion:	2004
Architects:	Tim Ronalds Architects
Client:	Hackney Empire

Lifts are an expected feature of most public buildings, including historic buildings that provide a service to the public. This includes old theatres and music halls, but these buildings present particular difficulties for the simple reason that audiences are seated on several levels, each often with a completely separate staircase. The purpose of the separation was to ensure that ticket holders restricted themselves to the area of seating they had paid for without 'mixing'. For example, the cost of seats in the stalls was more than the cost of seats or even standing in the upper circle known as the 'gods'.

The Hackney Empire theatre, opened in 1901, was typical of this arrangement, designed by Frank Matcham, an architect whose expertise was theatre design. A century later in 2001, the theatre decided to embark on a major upgrade of its facilities as part of a rescue plan to ensure the secure future of the building and its Grade II listing. Modern regulations, plus reliance in part on public funding, meant that twenty-first-century expectations for inclusive design would need to

Tickets for the circle cost more than the balcony, so to prevent 'mixing', the staircase to each was designed to be separate. This photograph shows the unchanged original staircases leading up to the separate levels.

be met, a commitment completely endorsed by the client. Up until 2001 the seating available for people unable to use stairs was confined to the front stalls. Reduced ticket prices acknowledged this limitation of choice. The promenade at the rear of the stalls included an audience bar, a key feature of the music hall tradition, and one also repeated on the upper tiers. However, for these there was no means of access other than by stairs; just one of the many challenges taken on by the project team.

The architect appointed in 2001 was asked to review options for resolving these limitations in order to maximize the audience experience for everyone. To complicate the brief yet further, many staff back-of-house activities were located on upper levels including the trustees' board room. Something had to be done!

This part of the project commenced with a detailed access audit of the building, noting in particular where the separate staircases could potentially link up and where a lift might be inserted. The lift would have to serve theatregoers, of course, but also staff and trustees. A possible location was identified that would provide sufficient room for one lift but not for two. Reliance on one lift with no alternative back-up usually raises concerns for lift failure, but given all the circumstances it was decided that the proposal should be pursued.

The new lift would need to convey people between three levels, two for theatregoers and another for staff and trustees. Usually, this type of requirement is addressed by installing a lift car with one door at the front and another opposite at the back. This arrangement is quite usual. However, at the Hackney Empire the lift would need to have its second door on an adjoining, not opposite wall, adding complexity to the lift mechanism and, of course, to cost. But the ingenuity of the proposal

was welcomed because it successfully addressed what otherwise would be a major shortcoming. Furthermore, once adopted, other accessible design issues regarding circulation were unlocked and fell into place.

In practice, the complexity of the lift design has meant that it has to be used with care and under supervision, with visitors escorted by staff. It has also meant that a back-up rescue plan from each upper level has had to be devised, not least for emergency escape. These are all matters that can be managed if routinely tested, ensuring that the best can be made of any limitations.

The new lift and a staircase are located at the rear of the theatre in the reconstructed pub. The lift is operated by staff and conveys wheelchair users – visitors, staff and trustees – to all upper levels.

Case Study: Queens House Greenwich, London

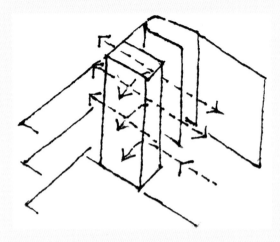

Insertion sketch for the Queen's House.

Project Details:	
Sector:	Museum
Location:	London
Completion:	2000
Architects:	Allies and Morrison
Client:	Royal Museums Greenwich

The Queen's House Greenwich has been much changed since its original design by Inigo Jones and, despite its title, it has rarely been used as a royal residence. For nearly a century it has instead been part of the National Maritime Museum along with its near neighbour, the Royal Observatory Greenwich. In the 1990s a decision was made to improve the museum's display areas in time for the Millennium celebrations in 2000. This project relied substantially on public funding which, combined with the expectations of the recently enacted Disability Discrimination Act of 1995, ensured that accessibility would be high on the agenda.

The formal steps up to the house entrance will be familiar to many and the ingenious changes made to achieve step-free access are described in Chapter 5. This section examines how a lift shaft was inserted into the building in order to provide internal step-free access between levels.

The principal staircase in the house is the Tulip Stairs, famous at the time for its structural innovation. But there are several other staircases, some of which are service stairs originally intended for use by servants. As is often the case with working stairs, these had been altered or replaced over the years. In terms of conservation, this makes such stairs potential candidates for change provided that there is a justifiable reason for doing so. In this case, the 'reason' was to replace the servants' stair with a new staircase and critically, a passenger lift.

There were two essential benefits to the staircase identified for this purpose. First, its consistent form and continuity from basement level up to the top floor of the building made it suitable for adaptation as a lift shaft. Second, its location would enable people using the new lift to travel from entrance level directly to a lobby serving major rooms and salons on each visitor level. These benefits were critical and cannot be overstated.

Having arrived at this point in the design decision process, the practicalities of available space had to be addressed. This required a degree of flexibility regarding minimum regulatory dimensions if the objective was to be achieved. The new stair design involved winding tapered steps that are common in older buildings but less common in new. However, with careful detailing, robustly fixed handrails and effective lighting, an acceptable solution was achieved.

In order to install a lift shaft and retain the stair-well as an important circulation route, the lift car had to be designed with the door on its long side rather than the more usual end-on position. The end-on position allows simple forward entry by a wheelchair user into the lift car, reversing out on arrival at the next floor. By contrast, side entry requires a different and more complex manoeuvre. This can be achieved, provided that the lift car door opening is wider than usual and to ensure this was possible, the lift car had to be a bespoke design.

The end result is a practical and acceptable solution to a difficult problem that required flexibility of thinking on the part of all involved. It enabled the museum to open its doors to all visitors, regardless of disability, in time for the Millennium celebrations.

The new lift shaft and new staircase had to fit neatly into the original service stairwell footprint. The stairs served all levels from basement to first floor.

The new lift takes visitors unable to use stairs from the new basement 'arrival' level up to the two levels above.

Case Study: Ashmolean Museum, Oxford

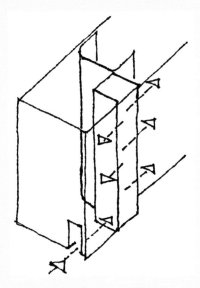

Insertion sketch for the Ashmolean Museum.

staff offices within a refurbished Taylor Institute wing, with its own entrance from St Giles. The brief to the architect required step-free accessibility for both visitors and staff, as would be expected of any modern public building.

Prior to these ambitious plans, step-free visitor access had been made possible from street to museum entrance level by the discrete construction of a ramp within the museum forecourt. From this point on, however, there were three key problems yet to be addressed. The first concerned onward circulation by visitors into the main galleries, at that

Project Details:	
Sector:	Museum
Location:	Oxford
Completion:	2009
Architects:	Rick Mather Architects
Client:	Ashmolean Museum of Art and Archaeology

The Ashmolean Museum building in Beaumont Street, Oxford, first opened in 1845, replacing the original buildings erected nearly 200 years previously. A century and a half later, in 2006, the university authorities decided on a phased programme of improvements aimed at doubling the display area and providing substantially improved facilities for visitors. These were to include a shop, more WC facilities, a café and a rooftop restaurant, all typically essential for meeting current visitor expectations. The project also set out to accommodate

The original stone staircase at the museum entrance lobby remains unchanged and is still in use.

time up and then down a short flight of steps, known as the Cockerell steps. For visitors unable to climb the steps, a long detour was necessary. Second, the only passenger lift available was located at the far end of the museum, a considerable distance from the museum entrance. And third was the task of aligning the three museum floor levels with the five new staff floor levels.

The last two problems concern us here since they were resolved by the insertion of a special lift. Given the considerable scale of the museum complex, two lifts would be essential for reasons of comfort and convenience. With the new lift supplementing the original, this problem was resolved. To address the problem of alignment, it was necessary for the new lift to serve three floors levels on one side and five on the other. This meant specifying a bespoke through-lift with two doors opposite each other, freely open for use by the public on one side but passcode operated by staff on the other.

The mechanics of the new lift car with opposing doors are relatively uncomplicated and work reliably. The only drawback is the combined heavy demand of both public and staff use, unavoidably leading to waiting at peak periods. This is especially the case for visitors visiting the roof terrace restaurant for coffee or tea. In all other respects the new lift is

This beautiful new staircase is at the heart of the refurbished museum and successfully uses daylight to provide drama where the new building connects with the old. The new lift to the right serves all public levels on the museum side and also all staff levels to the rear building. (Photo: © Andy Matthews)

an invaluable asset to a project that has received many awards for its ingenuity and successful transformation.

Chapter Eight

Reorientation

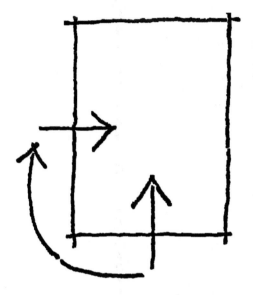

Reorientation sketch.

I T IS OFTEN THE CASE THAT THE MAIN entrance to an historic public building is up a flight of steps. Christ Church in Spitalfields is a case in point. Here, the steps are such an integral part of the building frontage, and such an obstacle to step-free access, that any effective change would be almost inconceivable.

In these situations it is worth considering reorientating the entrance to a less imposing elevation that can accommodate a new building element, such as a ramp. According to each circumstance, the ramp might go up or, as at Christ Church, it might go down. To enable such an option to work it must make sense with regard to internal circulation routes and add value to the project as a whole. At Spitalfields this was precisely the case. With a reorientated entrance made possible with a ramp, the new arrangement provides direct and more logical entry into the visitor facilities and using a new lift close by up to the areas of worship.

Main Case Study: Christ Church, Spitalfields, London

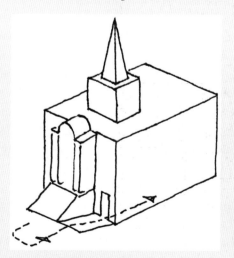

Reorientation sketch for Christ Church.

Project Details:	
Sector:	Place of Worship
Location:	London
Completion:	2015
Architects:	Dow Jones Architects
Client:	Friends of Christ Church Spitalfields

OPPOSITE: Christ Church in Spitalfields.

Historic Background

Christ Church Spitalfields was built in the early eighteenth century to a design by Nicholas Hawksmoor. Situated to the east of the City Of London, it is regarded by many as one of the finest of the 'Commissioners' Churches', so named after the Commission for Building Fifty New Churches, which had been established by an Act of Parliament in 1711. The purpose of the commission was to build churches to serve London's new settlements. In the event, only twelve of the planned fifty churches were built, of which six were designed by Hawksmoor. Christ Church was designated for an area dominated by Catholic Huguenots as a show of Anglican authority. The church is approached by a steep flight of steps leading to a magnificent porch beneath a broad tower topped by a distinctive steeple.

By the mid-twentieth century, Christ Church was nearly derelict and faced demolition. The Friends of Christ Church Spitalfields was formed to raise money and project-manage the restoration of the Grade I listed building. This ambitious project was finally completed in 2004, enabling a wide range of uses to run alongside Christ Church's primary function as a place of worship.

As part of the restoration process, the burial vaults beneath the church had to be cleared. The Friends of Christ Church raised funds for the employment of an archaeological team, who excavated nearly 1,000 interments. The project was written up as a landmark study, covering everything from mortuary practices to the causes of death of the local population.

In 2015 the crypt was restored, providing extensive facilities for the church's wide-reaching social programme, as well as taking the opportunity to provide step-free access to the crypt and to the magnificent church above. This review assesses the sensitive works done at this stage to provide a fully accessible design that respects and even enhances Hawksmoor's architecture.

As we see in other projects in this book, a thorough understanding of the significance of the historic

CHRIST CHURCH, SPITALFIELDS.
D D

A period view of the church from Spitalfields. (Image: Blomfield, Reginald Theodore, Sir, 1856–1942, Public domain, via Wikimedia Commons)

structure is essential if adaptations to improve access are to be successful. In the case of Christ Church, a gazetteer, based on site investigation and examination of archive materials, was produced by the Conservation Architect Oliver Caroe to describe and assess the significance of all parts of the crypt. This historic assessment was complemented by a full access audit, reviewing the journey to be taken to gain access to the crypt as well as the church above by anyone with a disability.

Case Study

At Christ Church, the issues confronting the architect were similar to those at Tate Britain and the

Fitzwilliam Museum. The dominant feature at the front of the church is the flight of steps rising several metres from pavement level into the church itself. Unusually, the steps have handrails to either side, but despite this benefit, they remain impossible for many people to climb. The church is on a busy main road and has, for many years, made use of its crypt for meetings and as the location of a café. The crypt was reached via a short flight of steps.

The church felt that better use of the crypt could be made if the facilities on offer for visitors could be upgraded. This would include a more ambitious kind of café selling hot food and more flexible meeting spaces backed up by improved toilet facilities. The church also wanted to ensure that everyone could benefit from these plans, not least older parishioners and others unable to climb steps. Given the contribution of public finances, careful thought was given to achieving step-free access into the church itself. For some years a rear service door had been relied on, requiring an escort on arrival. A better arrangement was sought, one more suited to modern expectations and less demanding of church personnel.

This was the brief for the architect in 2008. Clearly, getting into and out of the church and crypt were major challenges to be addressed both to satisfy the church but also legislation and public funding requirements. Given the Grade l listing, altering the front steps in any significant way would be out of the question. Instead, the entrance arrangement would need to be reorientated, in this case to the side yard. The difference in levels between pavement and crypt were still considerable but could be addressed by the installation of a long ramp.

A ramp was the option developed by the architect. Ingeniously commencing the ramp down from the church forecourt, it passes through the crypt entrance as it continues its downward slope to café level. At several points the ramp has to intersect with existing door openings that needed to be retained. This it does, providing an enticing view down into the café area as it progresses. The quality of materials and robust simple design of details mean the ramped solution works well.

The next challenge was to install a lift up into the church itself. The key here was for the lift to arrive at a location in the church that was practical and convenient but discrete. This was achieved by reconfiguring the existing rear escape staircase and lobby to accommodate a lift shaft. Again, this solution works well for both access and conservation.

Externally, entry into the church crypt is simple and self-evident, aligning with original door openings. Internally, the new lift is located out of view so it does not disturb the church interior. With high quality detailing and imaginatively illuminated spaces, client and visitors can all be pleased with the outcome.

The entrance steps have in the past had handrails added, but these are still difficult or impossible for some people. The steps remain unchanged, but churchgoers can now use a new lift from the crypt up to the main church level.

The Big Idea

The appraisal method here focuses on the intended means of entering the church, the front steps. These are such a significant element of the building that any intervention would be unwelcome and any solution to step-free access unlikely.

The architect chose to investigate the scope for reorientation by creating an alternative, step-free entrance into the church. There are potential pitfalls when developing alternative entrances, especially if perceived as a back-door or second-class entrance. However, if the alternative provides obvious benefits to all and adds value to the project aims, the concept is more likely to be viewed favourably.

Here, the step-free entrance is the route for everyone moving to the crypt area, which accommodates meeting rooms, café and bar and, of course, WCs. Critically, it is also the location decided on for the construction of a lift that provides access up to the main church level for worship.

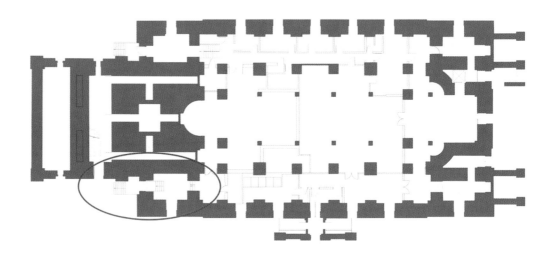

Plan showing original steps down to the crypt.

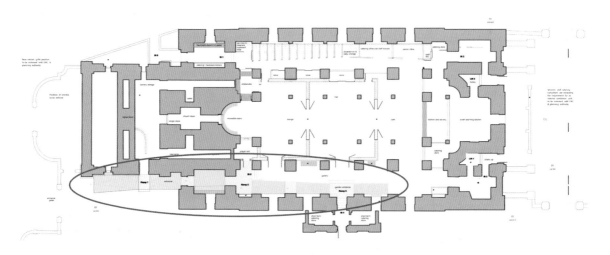

Plan showing the new ramp down into the crypt.

Looking at similar well-known buildings – St Paul's Cathedral in London included – it is wise to pause and investigate alternative options. Reorientation would be an apt suggestion and so too insertion. As with the option chosen at Christ Church, any design should be visually discrete as well as adding value to the project as a whole.

In summary, this brief analysis identifies two important points. First, explore by all means the ways of modifying the obvious obstacle to access, in this case the steps, but keep an open mind on alternative options. Second, where offering an alternative, its adoption as an idea increases as the benefits and practical value increase.

Arrival

The whole purpose of a public building is for the public to visit. Urban locations would seem best suited to this where reliance on public transport is concerned. This urban church is on a major bus route – all buses in London are accessible – with Whitechapel tube station close by. A further advantage is the location of Blue Badge parking immediately outside the church and also a taxi drop-off. Though no doubt outside of the direct influence of church authority, the local transport and the local highways department have provided the church with a major advantage at the outset with the provision of such excellent transport and access facilities.

Approach

A further benefit has been the local highways department decision to dispense with raised kerbs between road and pavement level, including a 'level' road crossing by the church itself. Combined with the reasonably even paved surfaces and abundant signage, the local context provides very supportive access indeed.

Curiously, the paved surface to the church front-age itself is less than ideal, formed as it is by small clay tiles laid in a diagonal pattern. These are almost certainly a recent addition and impede ease of movement for wheelchair users, children's buggies and people with poor balance. Granite slabs have been cut into the tiles like a cart track which helps, but a bolder, more effective solution would be justified for this significant building. The challenge here, as always, is to attempt to provide a seamless journey from street frontage to the building across property boundaries. This will usually require dogged persistence by the designer and 'buy in' from the local authority.

Entry to the crypt forecourt is across a cobbled yard currently in use as an external café space. This is curiously at odds with the crypt café offering but adds to the bustling street scene and is popular when weather permits.

What is helpful is that the distances from roadside to forecourt and onward to crypt entrance are short – always helpful – and enable a clear view of the

View of forecourt before work began showing what a neglected space it was. The forecourt is now an extension of the crypt café, making excellent use of what was previously a neglected area.

'journey' involved. Direction to the crypt entrance relies, however, on an A-board sign, a potential obstacle in the forecourt for blind people. An alternative is difficult to conceive and is a worthy street design challenge in itself.

Entry

The church entrance is unmistakably via the front steps, so conveying information regarding the step-free alternative via the crypt lift is critical. This too is a design challenge given the natural reluctance to displaying signage on historic buildings. In this case, a modest sign is displayed but it is easy to miss.

On approach, the first section of entrance ramp is clear, visually defined by hand rails and leads directly to a level landing directly in front of the crypt entrance. Black painted drainage grills help emphasize the landing, a good example of added value from an essential design component.

On entry, the ramp continues its descent to café level, intersecting at landing points with existing door openings. For this reason the ramp sections are of slightly differing gradients but given the benefits, this is quite acceptable. Noticeable throughout is the robust ramp handrail and balustrade design, well suited to this robust crypt space.

The ramp is now a major feature of the entry corridor to the crypt café and conference areas. It is generous enough for multiple users at one time and, positioned directly alongside an adjoining stepped corridor, it ensures no separation of visitors on entry. On the contrary, this space works well for both people movement and the presentation of information in gallery style.

The Café and Meeting Rooms

Although unlit by daylight, these spaces seem full of light, albeit by artificial up-lighting of the vaults.

The crypt-level entrance is approached by the new ramp leading down to a doorway, with intermediate landings en route. The new railings are robust and well detailed, emulating the qualities of the historic front gates.

The crypt area is a flexible space allowing the café to be opened or closed from the meeting rooms. These have acoustic curtains and folding doors to minimize any disturbance.

The tendency of acoustic echo in such spaces is here attenuated by generous full-height curtains hung on walls. Given the generosity of space available and an uncluttered layout, movement is comfortably achieved even for wheelchair users.

Doorways are kept to a minimum, with flexibility of use as a priority. All are generously wide, though some would benefit from bolder manifestation to the glazing panels in order to make them more discernable for blind and partially-sighted people.

To the rear of the main space is a corridor where WCs are located, with the usual unisex wheelchair-accessible WC closest by. Opening large cubicle doors into the corridor can cause obstructions, but is here overcome by the use of a sliding door. There are mixed views about such doors since while they resolve the potential for obstructing a corridor, they can be difficult to slide open unless fitted with a superior slide mechanism.

The Lift

A major component of this project is the provision of lift access from crypt level up to the main church level above. For practical reasons on the upper floor, the lift is located to the rear of the café area at the far end of the circulation corridor. It is easy to miss and located as it is to the rear, it appears to be for private rather than public use.

This points out the difficulty of how best to display essential signage – to the lift in this case – without it being overbearing.

Escape

For simplicity, it is always preferable for the way into a building to be the way out. This is even more the case for emergency escape. Here, the daylight through the door opening leaves no doubt about which direction to leave in an emergency.

The new lift entrance can be seen at the end of this corridor. The lift takes visitors directly to the main level of the church above.

View of the ramp back to the crypt entrance from the café. This ramp provides step-free entry in and out, including in an emergency escape situation.

Case Study: Tate Britain, London

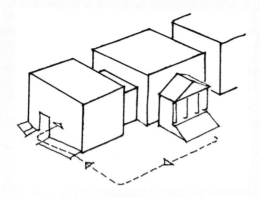

Reorientation sketch for Tate Britain.

Project Details:	
Sector:	Gallery
Location:	London
Completion:	2001
Architects:	Allies and Morrison
Client:	Tate Britain

Many visitors to London will be familiar with the riverside view of Tate Britain, especially its unusually grand and imposing entrance staircase. Until recently this was the main entrance for the visiting public, providing a sense of occasion on entry into the building and a wonderful view of the Thames on exit. For gallery staff, this was not the case; they instead entered the building at the rear via a simple, almost level route and for many years this was the route in for visiting wheelchair users.

In 1987 James Stirling designed the Clore Gallery located to the east as a new wing. This building provided step-free entry but with a circuitous internal route into the main gallery area, including a lift. A decade later a new more ambitious project was commissioned with a part of its brief calling for a step-free entrance that could deliver visitors right to the heart of the building. This was a combined undertaking with one architect to reconfigure the gallery internally and another to design external approaches and entry.

No amount of ingenuity could make the original front steps accessible and instead, the bold decision was made to reorientate the new Manton entrance to the elevation in Atterbury Street. This major decision did not in itself achieve step-free access, but it did allow a new entrance ramp and steps to resolve the difference in levels between outside and in. It also made sense for two other reasons. First, the new entrance was directly positioned on the route serving the nearest tube station at Pimlico, a route that most visitors use. Second, it

The new entry point is reorientated from the riverfront to Atterbury Street, the direction of arrival for most visitors. The long but gentle ramp leads to the lower ground level entrance, with foyer, shops and café encountered on arrival.

provided an opportunity to create several on-street Blue Badge parking bays for disabled visitors right beside the ramp.

This logic improved arrangements for arrival externally and was matched internally by delivering visitors directly into a generous new reception area, a large café with WC facilities close by and, of course, a shop. As a package, these changes have transformed access into the gallery. The grand scale of the building means that it is well able to accommodate the changes with ease.

The original front steps remain unchanged, thereby retaining the familiar frontage. However, they are now more usually occupied by seated visitors, enjoying the river views and eating their sandwiches.

The original and dominant front entrance and steps remain unaltered. They still provide excellent raised views across the Thames, so enjoyed by visitors. (Photo: Rept0n1x, CC BY-SA 3, via Wikimedia Commons)

Case Study: Fitzwilliam Museum, Cambridge

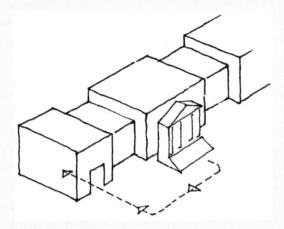

Reorientation sketch for the Fitzwilliam Museum.

Project Details:	
Sector:	Museum
Location:	Cambridge
Completion:	2004
Architects:	John Miller & Partners
Client:	The University of Cambridge

This impressive Grade 1 listed building sits back from Fitzwilliam Street in Cambridge, sited in its own grounds. The central Palladian pavilion of 1848 once stood alone but wings were added in 1931 to provide additional space for exhibitions. Entry into the main pavilion is up a broad flight of portico steps bringing visitors into a spectacular entrance hall with a grand staircase to the upper galleries.

The museum was free to enter from the outset and in that spirit plans were made in 2004 to improve facilities for the increasing number of visitors and school parties and to expand exhibition space yet further. Part of the architect's brief was to ensure that the proposals could provide suitable step-free entry, together with vertical circulation by lift.

As with other similar buildings, the entrance steps are a formidable challenge for some, but they are such an integral part of the design that any significant physical change would be unacceptable. The decision was therefore made to reorientate the entrance by creating a new way into the museum via one of the wings. This option offered several advantages. Its location is directly opposite the entry point onto the site, providing a clear and direct route to the new step-free entrance as an alternative to the portico steps.

To maximize these advantages, the architect located a reception desk, cloaks and WCs at the

In this case study the entrance has been reorientated to the left pavilion, directly in front of the visitor arrival point at street level. Once within the building, visitors move on via a new staircase or by lift to the main gallery levels.

entry point, before visitors move along the wing to the exhibition spaces themselves. This design decision is important since it quickly draws visitors away from any congestion, incentivized in this case by a view of the café area and shop.

To avoid any need to use the grand staircase, a new flight is provided in the wing. In addition, a clearly visible free-standing passenger lift has been installed in what was previously an open service yard, now glazed over. The combination of daylight, activity and clear direction has made this project very successful in terms of accessibility. Furthermore, with these improvements in place, the museum has, like so many spacious public buildings, needed little other change.

The grand entrance involves negotiating steps both at the gateway and also up the portico steps. The original entrance remains unchanged and is still in use, though most visitors will arrive from the new entrance, thereby reaching the spectacular higher level foyer as part of their journey through the gallery.

Case Study: The Royal Albert Memorial Museum, Exeter

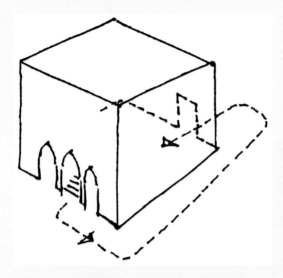

Reorientation sketch for the Exeter RAMM.

Project Details:	
Sector:	Museum
Location:	Exeter
Completion:	2012
Architects:	Allies and Morrison
Client:	The Royal Albert Memorial Museum

The Royal Albert Memorial Museum (RAMM) in Exeter, a regional outpost of the Victoria & Albert Museum in London, was created in 1868. This important public museum later received royal patronage. The building is listed and plays an important role in the educational activities of the area. Given its age and its patron, the building style is unapologetically Victorian. It sits on a sloping site, never a problem for the Victorians, with a stepped entrance leading into a stepped reception foyer and onward staircases up and down to the museum's various facilities.

A major decision to substantially upgrade the museum using public funds was made in 2007. The aim was to increase exhibition space and educational facilities along with expanded café and shop and service support areas. An early challenge was for the architect to devise a solution to step-free entry and ease of circulation throughout the museum. The existing adaptations to the stepped entrance and foyer relied on a single platform lift for step-free entry. The unreliability of these devices was just one of several reasons for exploring alternative options.

To address this ambition, the architect and client chose to avoid any major and possibly unacceptable intervention to the stepped front entrance and foyer. Instead, it was proposed that the step-free entry would be achieved by reorientating to the rear of the building, in effect creating two entrances. This decision was entirely practical, partly in response to the conservation issues involved but also given the hilly local topography and the complete absence of on-street car parking nearby.

Developing the rear entrance option had the key benefit of providing secure Blue Badge car parking for disabled visitors, with direct and level entry into the museum. Importantly, this route delivers the visitor not into a back corridor but directly into a new foyer area with a ticketing desk and a bookshop. Ingeniously, the connection between the old building and the new is readily identified by a glazed connection referred to as the 'slot'. This feature, with daylight penetrating into the building, greatly assists with internal wayfinding. Onward

Disabled visitors to the reorientated new entrance at the rear are now able to park their car in a designated parking space. They can then either enter using a gentle ramp or, if preferred, climb the easy-going steps to the main foyer.

access is clearly signed to a new lift, visitor WCs and cloakroom facilities. This is most important if the new reorientated way in is to be seen as a new entrance in its own right, rather than as a secondary or, worse still, inconvenient back door requiring staff escort.

The overall impression on arrival is of a well-designed, well-maintained and convenient way in to the museum, which together provides a welcome alternative to the far less convenient stepped on-street entrance.

In 2012, RAMM was named the United Kingdom's 'Museum of the Year' by The Art Fund charity, which cited its 'ambition and imagination'. In the same year, it was honoured with the American Event Design Award for Best Museum Environment (2012) and since then, it has won over a dozen other awards, including three regional RIBA awards (2013) and the Collections Trust award, which recognized the curatorial and collections management good practice carried out by the museum (2013).

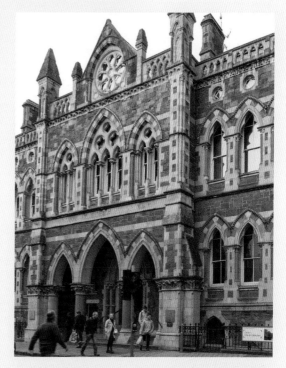

The original stepped entrance from street level, previously supplemented by a platform lift, remains in use. There is no on-street parking close by, making the new car park entrance a considerable asset for disabled visitors. (Photo: Pymouss - Own work, CC BY-SA 4.0, via Wikimedia Commons)

Case Study: Royal Festival Hall, London

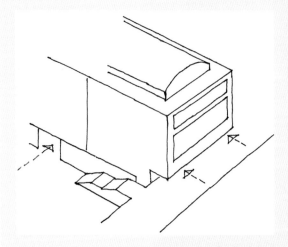

Reorientation sketch for the Royal Festival Hall.

Project Details:	
Sector:	Culture
Location:	London
Completion:	2008
Architects:	Allies and Morrison
Client:	Southbank Centre

The Royal Festival Hall (RFH) first opened in 1951 as the centrepiece of the Festival of Britain celebrations on London's Southbank. Its fresh modern appearance took full advantage of its Thames-side location looking north across the river towards Westminster and the City of London. It was originally conceived that the concert hall building would be entered on either side, upstream to the east and downstream to the west.

In 1964 the original building frontage was extended by the addition of a new riverside entrance accessed by a vehicular service road. Concertgoers would now be able to arrive in their cars to a new lower foyer with stairs and a lift connecting to the main foyer level above. The service road, over time, came to provide informal disabled visitor parking, with considerable space set aside in the evenings for this purpose. With step-free access into the building and a lift connecting lower to upper foyers, this arrangement worked. However, the lift was too small by current standards and so too the lobbies, and both proved inadequate at peak periods.

In 2005 the RFH embarked on a major upgrade that set out to reduce peak period pressure on the riverside entrance and, at the same time, to exploit the commercial potential of the river embankment for retail outlets, new restaurants and cafés. This involved reorientating the entry points away from the river and returning them once again to east and west.

These newly created commercial facilities on the Embankment were designed as pedestrian spaces and could no longer provide access for vehicles. This meant that the 'informal' disabled parking arrangement had to be withdrawn. It was a client condition that a new permanent parking facility had to be created in order to compensate. Critically, it would have to include step-free access to the main upper foyer if it was to be considered acceptable. Fortunately, this became possible by incorporating Blue Badge bays into a new visitor car park adjacent to the step-free west entrance. This decision restored accessibility into the building, but there were internal complexities to be resolved.

Entry at this point did not include internal lift access to the concert hall foyer level above, meaning that a new internal lift on that side would

The original entrance has been brought back into use, critically providing step-free access from street level. Purpose-designed Blue Badge parking has been provided close by and on entry. Concertgoers now have direct access to all concert hall levels above using the new lift.

be essential. Similarly, a new external lift would also be required to provide access from road level up to the riverside cafés and shops. These were both major undertakings committed to by the client and the funders and have achieved a standard of accessibility that should serve the Festival Hall and its many disabled visitors well for years to come.

The riverside terrace is now devoted to visitors enjoying the shops and cafés. Concertgoers can also enter here, using the new lift for access to the concert hall levels above.

Case Study: Ironmonger Row Swimming Baths, Finsbury, London

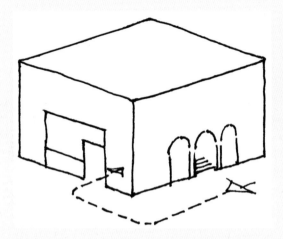

Reorientation sketch for Ironmonger Row.

Project Details:

Sector:	Leisure
Location:	London
Completion:	2013
Architects:	Tim Ronalds Architects
Client:	Islington Council

The Ironmonger Row Baths were built in 1931 by the London Borough of Finsbury as part of a national drive for improved health through exercise at that time. It was widely renowned for its competition-standard pool with high diving board. In addition, it set out to serve the local community by the provision of public 'slipper' baths, a public laundry and Turkish Bath facilities that made provision for women as well as men. The building was listed Grade II in 2006.

In the spirit of its conception as public baths, the brief for a major upgrade in 2009 included access for all regardless of disability. This aspiration was backed up by full client support for inclusive design, including the appointment of an access liaison officer and the formation of an access group of local residents with disabilities to act as a sounding board for ideas.

With this brief, the architect faced a range of challenges, among which was how to design a new step-free public entrance. The original entrance

The original entrance is stepped, with a further flight of steps immediately inside. Other than the stone plaque above the door, it can be passed by almost unnoticed by visitors.

involved steps up from pavement level taking visitors into an atmospheric but tightly planned reception lobby with yet further steps to the pools. The listed status and confined spaces limited scope for major alterations both inside and out. Instead, a key decision was made to reorientate by creating a new entrance to the south.

On the south side the architect was able to create a handsome, generous and step-free entrance linked directly to the new, reconfigured internal circulation. The new entrance now leads directly into a generous reception area adjacent to a visitor café with step-free onward access to changing rooms and the pools. The upper-level viewing galleries and new gym facilities are now all accessed by a lift rather than just stairs as before. This change also offered a welcome opportunity for providing some on-street Blue Badge disabled parking bays close by.

The client's commitment and the effort by the architect have been rewarded by considerable national praise and continued thriving local support. The pool was for some years a training facility for the UK Olympic swimming team and more recently for the Paralympic swimming team.

This handsome reorientated new entrance proudly proclaims its purpose. It is level and leads directly to a new reception foyer and the pool changing rooms.

Mechanization

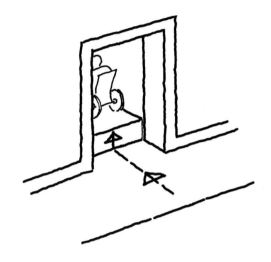

Mechanization sketch.

MOVEMENT WITHIN A BUILDING USING mechanization is far from unusual, most usually encountered as passenger lifts for vertical movement between floor levels. Sometimes it takes the form of travelators for long distance horizontal movement in large airports or for inclined movement in shopping centres. Only occasionally is the means of entry into a building directly from the street reliant on mechanized movement. This chapter looks at some examples, all listed buildings and all as an alternative to the existing stepped entrances that have had insufficient scope for alteration.

In all the examples the intention has been to achieve step-free access at the 'front door' but with the important proviso that the change should, visually at least, be barely evident in order to satisfy conservation concerns for unchanged appearance.

The examples rely on just two forms of mechanized lifting. The first and more usual is the use of platform lifts relying on combinations of cogs, screws and levers driven by an electric motor. Unfairly or otherwise,

these have a reputation for unreliability, often arising from misuse or lack of maintenance. The second type is more elaborate, and therefore more expensive, and relies on hydraulic pumps to reconfigure steps to lifting mode and then return to steps again.

Whereas platform lifts have to be sheltered from weather, hydraulic steps can be exposed. This does incur a cost for regular cleaning and maintenance but given that, they are reliable.

Main Case Study: The Institution of Civil Engineers, London

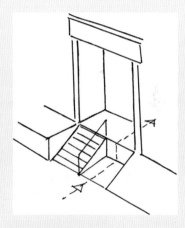

Mechanization sketch for ICE.

Project Details:	
Sector:	Headquarters
Location:	London
Completion:	2016
Architects:	Feilden+Mawson
Client:	ICE

OPPOSITE: The Institution of Civil Engineers in Westminster.

Historic Background

The Grade ll listed Institution of Civil Engineers (ICE) was designed in the early twentieth century by James Miller, a Scottish architect, who was recognized for his commercial architecture in Glasgow and for his Scottish railway stations. In 1910 he won the competition to design the ICE headquarters at One Great George Street, Westminster. At the same time he designed the matching extension to the adjoining Institution of Mechanical Engineers. ICE was founded by engineers in 1818; its first president was Thomas Telford.

The institution occupies a key corner site on the route from St James's Park to Parliament Square, its solid Portland stone, slate roof and neo-Baroque detailing competing in grandeur with other imposing government buildings in the area. The building's central Ionic columned portal is surmounted by an elaborately carved crest. Internally, the institution is equally significant, its domed assembly hall and other rooms adorned with rich detailing.

The challenge here was to modify the steps to provide step-free access.

Case Study

The headquarters of ICE has a prominent location just off Parliament Square, facing the Treasury. Given its comprehensive conference facilities and close location to government, the institution gains valuable income from these activities. To expand this benefit, it was considered essential to meet current expectations with regard to inclusive design. The most obvious shortcoming was the absence of step-free entry into the building. Its main entrance, as with the Treasury on Whitehall, involved two flights of steps connected half way by a landing. For some years a holding measure was in place – a rear service door was used by wheelchair users – but this was no longer considered acceptable. Instead, a 'front door' approach had to be explored and this was the architect's brief.

Constructing a suitable ramp would be impossible given the length required and the limited space available. Other options were considered, all of them mechanical employing vertical platform lifts, both outside and inside the building, but none of them at this early stage set out to modify the seemingly impossible front steps. However, the architects finally confronted the impossible head on.

The photographs here show how the steps withdraw to reveal a platform lift that conveys the wheelchair user up to landing level. This sequence is repeated to another flight, finally arriving at the main entry level. The final photograph shows the wheelchair user leaving the building in reverse sequence.

The Big Idea

A helpful feature of the steps was their generous width. This arises from their dual function as a final escape exit as well as an entrance, suggesting that one side of the steps might be mechanized with the other side remaining unchanged. While a novel idea, it was not unique, so the institution took the bold decision to proceed with developing this option further.

Half the original steps on the right were removed and replaced by a lift installation designed to minimize any visual impact to this Grade II frontage.

How the steps 'move' is best described by comparing them to a chest of drawers where each drawer is pulled out sufficiently to form a step. At a touch of a button, all the 'drawers' close to reveal a platform lift able to rise up to the next level. After a wheelchair user has used the platform lift, the steps then return to their original position. The whole system is powered by hydraulic pumps located nearby that are unseen and unheard. The whole process of entry takes a relatively short time, but during this time, continued movement in and out of the building by others using the retained steps is unhindered.

Entrance

The means of entry is described above but for a first-time visitor a keen eye is required to see the call point at the bottom of the ICE front steps at pavement level. Pressing the button readily gains the attention of foyer staff who will then 'prepare' the automated steps for use. The staff are used to operating the steps but the visitor may not be, in which case the experience can be one of slight awkwardness or more likely, sheer delight.

Circulation

As with many other buildings of this type and period, once inside, the facilities in many ways already meet basic access requirements. The building has two good quality lifts serving all levels, generous circulation areas and accessible facilities. Above all, the high levels of staffing and management ensure that the needs of disabled conference attendees can be addressed, including explaining arrangements for emergency escape.

Conclusion

The automated steps at ICE no doubt required a generous budget but they should, over time, pay back as an investment, given the income-earning benefits they have brought. It is also the case with this building that most other access expectations were already in place, thereby easing the capital outlay. It befits an institution focused on promoting engineering to have such a well-engineered solution to inclusive design.

Case Study: Supreme Court, London

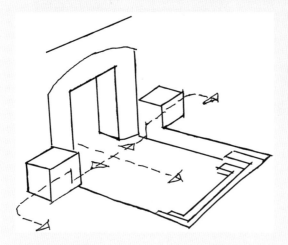

Mechanization sketch for the Supreme Court.

Project Details:	
Sector:	Government
Location:	London
Completion:	2009
Architects:	Feilden+Mawson
Client:	Ministry of Justice

The alterations to Gibson's Middlesex Town Hall on Parliament Square began in 2007, following the decision to change its use from a Crown Court to the Supreme Court, the highest court in the land. One of the many challenges to this change was to reverse the original physical restrictions to public access and create a building with an 'open door' policy. Part of the refurbishment brief was to facilitate public access to the court's proceedings with no limitations arising from disability. This commitment was to apply not just to areas intended for the visiting public, but also to those back-of-house areas for the judges and their staff, including changing rooms, meeting rooms, offices and a library.

Such a commitment would have to be visually evident at the point of entry fronting Parliament Square; providing a 'back-door' accessible entrance would simply not do. At first sight this appeared straightforward since the entrance door has level access from the pavement. However, inside the entrance foyer has three steps up to the main ground floor with reception, cloaks and lifts at that level. Some means had to be devised for overcoming those steps which, for ceremonial and conservation reasons, needed to remain. With a relatively small difference in levels, less than 500mm in this case, it is usual to first consider a ramp as a solution. But ramps with landings at top and bottom occupy considerable space, too much for the modest entrance foyer to accommodate.

What was evident, however, were the small porters' cubicles, one on either side of the entrance

The Supreme Court entrance is at pavement level, but as can be seen in this photograph there are foyer steps beyond. The challenge here was to devise step-free access between the upper and lower foyer levels. Given the relatively small lower foyer space, a ramp was not possible. (Photo: © chris2766/ Adobe Stock)

The solution was to modify each of the porter's rooms on either side of the entrance to accommodate platform lifts. This photograph shows a wheelchair user leaving one of the platform lifts at the upper foyer level.

lobby. The size of these was sufficient to install bespoke platform lifts and this was the design option adopted. They offered several advantages. The platform lifts could be installed into the original lobby structure with little visual evidence of change. In addition, with two lifts – one on either side for entrance and exit – the usual concerns for lift failure could be addressed. Critically, this arrangement would in no way impinge on what was already a foyer under pressure for accommodating ceremonial entrances.

As is often the case with buildings of this period, once at main ground floor level, front-of-house arrangements for accessibility were relatively straightforward. These included upgrading the two existing passenger lifts, one for the public and the other for staff, and adding accessible WC facilities for each. But one further issue had to be addressed, namely achieving step-free entry into the central courtroom. Whereas judges and the legal teams enter at a lower level, the public enters via doors on either side of the courtroom with a half flight of steps up to the viewing galleries. Retaining the steps on one side allowed the other flight to be replaced by a gated platform lift for wheelchair users. This replacement was sympathetically achieved through the use of quality materials such as carpeted floor covering and polished timber rails. This addressed the requirements for step-free access but in practice, the lift gates can be unreliable and require careful attention.

Case Study: The Treasury – the Whitehall entrance, London

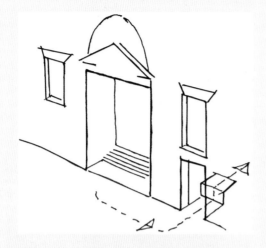

Mechanization sketch for the Treasury.

Project Details:	
Sector:	Government
Location:	London
Completion:	2002
Architects:	Foster+Partners
Client:	HM Treasury

Like all government offices in Whitehall, the Treasury is a large and complex building accommodating a great number of civil servants, senior officials and government ministers. All these buildings share a common interest in security such that the Treasury has just two entrances onto the public highway. One is in St James's and the other on Whitehall and it is this entrance that is our case study here.

The Whitehall entrance is stepped both from street level to foyer level and then again from foyer to ground floor where onward circulation by lifts and stairs begins. Given the client brief regarding inclusive design, the architect had to devise some

means of step-free entry that would be practical and would satisfy concerns for building conservation.

Unlike the St James's entrance where there was ample frontage to construct a ramp, no similar opportunity exists in Whitehall. Instead, attention moved to entering the building directly from the pavement using some form of powered mechanism. A detailed survey identified a small porters' space internally to one side of the inset arched entrance opening. It furthermore confirmed that

The steps at the Whitehall entrance discharge directly onto the public pavement with no space to construct a ramp. Instead, a lift has been installed to direct pavement level, seen to the right of the main entrance.

a small shaft could be cut through the floor slab at this point for a platform lift to 'arrive' at street level.

While this proposal looked feasible, a decision was needed as to how best to form a door opening at pavement level to serve the lift. Visually, this would need to be as discrete as possible, ideally located below the foyer window. This was achieved by carefully cutting out the window apron to provide a suitable opening. The result is an intervention that is barely noticed by the passer-by. While this 'invisibility' might not be suited to a public building, it works perfectly well for a place of employment where staff routinely come and go. It also works well because foyer security staff are always on duty and able to assist.

The end result is step-free entry that successfully enables disabled employees to enter and leave the building. At this point the employee must then move across the foyer to a second 'open' platform lift to get to the main ground floor level and onwards to their place of work. The effort and ingenuity necessary to install these high quality lifts are wholly justified, given that accessibility throughout is fully addressed by the wider upgrade project.

To gain access to the lift an opening had to be carefully cut into the original stonework, directly below an existing window.

Case Study: Buckingham Palace, London

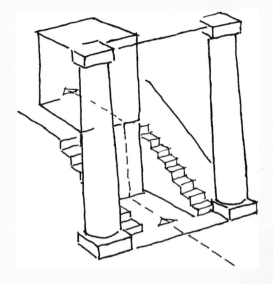

Mechanization sketch for Buckingham Palace.

Project Details:	
Sector:	Historic
Location:	London
Client:	The Royal Household Property Section

All visitor entrances into Buckingham Palace are designed to be imposing, not just by their scale and form but also by the use of steps. The public have for many years been able to tour the Palace, though wheelchair users must enter using a separate step-free route that detours from the grand entrance.

For invited functions like the annual Investiture, it is different. All guests arrive together at the quadrangle and enter into the Grand Hall via the Porte Cochere stairs. The three staircases allow several hundred waiting visitors to quickly move into the building and onto the event where honours are conferred. For wheelchair users it is not possible to use the steps so special arrangements are brought into operation each year when the events season begins.

One set of the Cochere steps are dismantled and stored away and in its place a bespoke platform lift is installed directly from the quadrangle level. The lift delivers the visitor to the upper level of the Marble Hall, enabling them to rejoin their friends and families there. This arrangement is

To the right of the photograph can be seen one of the entry staircases from quadrangle level into the Grand Hall above.

highly organized and with the lift operated by well-trained staff, it is usually faultless. At the end of the season the lift is removed and the steps once again reassembled in their original position with no trace of change. The lift can only convey one wheelchair user at a time, taking several minutes to do so. Given the excitement of the occasion, no one minds waiting, but in practice, queues of waiting wheelchair users can occur.

All these examples demonstrate the effort and commitment given by many national but also local institutions to resolving problems of inaccessibility. As time goes by, expectations for improved accessibility will increase and it can be anticipated that ever more clever mechanized solutions will feature as a key part of these improvements.

For the visitor season at the palace, half of the steps are removed and replaced by a platform lift. This provides step-free access, enabling participation for everyone at palace events.

Chapter Ten

Consultation

Origins

Consultation requires time and energy if it is to be useful and beneficial and if it is neither of these, it will be either avoided or ignored. It is, of course, part of any architect's scope of services to consult with individuals or groups representing the client's interests. The objective is to gain a clear understanding of expectations as to how a building will need to function. In architectural history there are many well-recorded accounts of prolonged and difficult consultation. Christopher Wren spent years of negotiation with the cathedral commissioners when designing St Paul's Cathedral and John Soane travelled long distances to have consultation meetings with his clients, often arriving – no doubt to their surprise – at breakfast time.

Historically, buildings specifically for disabled people were most likely to be hospitals. With Wren, the most notable was the Royal Naval Hospital in Greenwich and with Soane, the Chelsea Hospital in Westminster. The hospital commissioners were generally retired military with experience of how such buildings would need to function. Whether or not rank and file personnel were consulted on their design is doubtful, given the physical obstacles to mobility that were built in.

Consulting more widely other than with the client probably did not happen much at all. But when in 1947 the Town and Country Planning Act came into force it swept in change. The notion of planning consent from the local authority dictated that local people affected by an application for approval should, through consultation, be part of the consenting

Originally designed as the Royal Naval Hospital by Christopher Wren, it is now a fully accessible campus for the University of Greenwich.

OPPOSITE: The Coliseum in London's West End.

process. Disabled people were not excluded from this process, though in effect, the practicalities of engagement were not in place.

The first proposal for ensuring that disabled people should be consulted in the planning process was instead one of the aims of the Chronically Sick and Disabled Person's Act 1970. The importance of this piece of legislation cannot be overstated since for the first time it was officially recognized that the way in which buildings were designed could have a significant impact on disabled people's lives. Additional legislation soon followed that required local authorities to make provision for disabled people to be co-opted onto planning and other council committees so that their voice might be heard.

The legislation met with muted enthusiasm, partly no doubt because finding disabled people who were able and sufficiently organized to take part was problematic. This would only change after disability groups came into being in order to respond, a process that would take several years. Nevertheless, this was an important start to the development of consultation with disabled people as a process and to the development of support for those willing and able to take part.

An underlying problem, however, was that there was no clear or widely accepted understanding of what disabled people might need from buildings and no financial incentives to meet those needs. But a door had been opened and disabled activists often found encouragement at local level to get organized using existing groups representing disabled people's interests. This might be described as the emergence of a network of local disabled access groups united by a widely shared objective. They were committed to changing the way buildings were designed in order to ensure they could be used by everyone regardless of disability. The relevance of this to specific activities like education and employment are clear, but it also touched on places of culture and entertainment.

It took until 1981 before the aspiration for improved access to buildings gained international interest. That year was designated the International

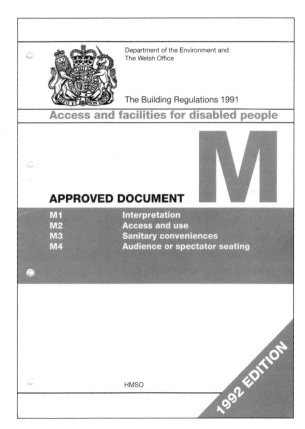

The first edition of *Approved Document M* 1985 set out exactly what was expected in order for a building to be considered accessible. This 1992 edition is part of a series of updated versions, the most recent published in 2015.

Year of Disabled People with the UK as co-sponsor. Government support and interest was therefore assured, but so also was royal support through the Prince of Wales Advisory Group on Disability. Interest in the circumstances of disabled people by the royal family was far from new, but the International Year of 1981 gave this broad interest a clear focus. Critically, the Prince's group firmly endorsed the relevance and importance of consulting with disabled people on matters directly affecting them. Disabled people were referred to in the group's report of 1983 as service 'consumers', thereby conferring a right to consultation.

Royal initiatives do not go unnoticed by government and in 1984 the Department for Health and Social Services also urged that consultation processes with disabled consumers should be put in place. With regard to buildings, a small group of architects, including Wycliffe Noble and Selwyn Goldsmith, helped draft the first guidance notes on what might make a building accessible. This led directly to the publication of national standards on accessibility for disabled people in the building regulations of 1985. Meeting these standards was not optional but a requirement. For the moment the limitations of legislation and regulations were that they did not apply to existing buildings unless they were significantly altered or improved.

All the necessary building blocks were now in place – legislation, regulations and expectations. But two things were missing: first, financial support and incentives to follow through, and second, introducing

The Citizen's Charter
and
People with Disabilities

A Checklist ✓

RAISING THE STANDARD

The Citizen's Charter paid particular attention to the rights of disabled people, including the suggestion that all town halls, old and new, should be audited with regard to accessibility.

consultation into the design process. Arguably, both these limitations were first addressed by what became known as the Citizen's Charter of 1991. Broadly speaking, this envisioned a contract between the citizen as consumer who, even if they had not contributed directly through taxation, had a right to public services. This political idea was firmly aimed at local authorities and it is no surprise that most local services derived in some way from the local town hall. This begged the question of whether or not everyone could physically manage to enter a town hall in the first place. Most town halls were old, sometimes of historic significance or even listed, and the answer in most cases was 'no'.

The Charter went on to add considerable emphasis to the importance of consulting with disabled people on how limitations of accessibility might be overcome. Local authorities were expected to respond and many did so, introducing ramps and other means of achieving step-free access to their town halls. This early flourish of interest might be considered the beginnings of a wider interest by architects in adapting historic buildings to the new demands of accessibility.

Local authorities had their own resources for undertaking these works; never enough of course, but some good work was done, setting an example for others in the profession to follow. However, this did present those responsible for the conservation of historic buildings with a dilemma – just how far could one alter a building in response to the aims of accessibility?

By 1995 the need for authoritative advice was urgent, driven by a new, more demanding piece of legislation, the Disability Discrimination Act, referred to in detail in an earlier chapter. The Act required that over a limited period of time any building offering a service to the public should ensure that the service was accessible for disabled people. While many services could be provided to a person at their home, this was not the case for museums, theatres, teaching institutions, places of worship and more. These buildings would have to adapt, raising three

In response to the Citizen's Charter, this access ramp was constructed in front of Islington Town Hall in 1992 to provide step-free access.

questions: how was this to be done, who could be consulted to establish priorities and who would pay?

Chapter 1 describes the legal duties of those responsible for change, but it fell to English Heritage, now Historic England, to advise how change might be acceptably achieved. This was set out in their important and timely publication of 1995 entitled, *Access to Historic Buildings*. But conflict was bound to arise, and did, between conservation experts wanting to minimize the need for alterations to historic fabric on the one hand, and disabled 'consumers' setting out their ambitions on the other. This potentially difficult situation gave rise to the employment of access consultants as a new kind of expert whose role was to steer a successful course between client and consumer. But it also gave rise to the interest by ACE, who published guidance on the subject of what should be aimed for and, just as important, it provided funds for doing so as a condition of receiving a project grant. This model was soon to be followed by the HLF, the Museums and Galleries Commission and similar institutions.

The introduction of accessibility as a criterion for lottery grant approval was the magic wand that was so much required at this point in time. It enabled the aims of legislation to be acted on by those responsible

Easy Access to Historic Properties 1995. This slim document was a breakthrough for building conservation experts to understand how alterations for improved accessibility could be acceptably implemented. It has been revised on several occasions since first published, the latest edition being 2015.

for our historic buildings. It provided the stimulus of funding for architects to develop ideas and ensured that institutions like English Heritage, previously rather shy on this subject, had to provide practical guidance.

Consultation Benefits and Methods

Gathering a group of people together over tea and cakes will always be enjoyable. But repeat this exercise where the people are all disabled and the shared topic is 'your favourite historic building' and the outcome is bound to be interesting as well. Better still, if that conversation is structured around 'your visit to your favourite historic building', exploring how each person travelled there, the arrangements on arrival, the customer experience, and so on. Have your notebook ready because it will be insightful and fruitful. This is the purpose of structured consultation, to draw on the personal experiences of visitors regarding their use of the building in order to understand difficulties encountered and, perhaps, how they might be addressed. It is not possible except in a generalized way to undertake a similar exercise for a proposed new building, but it is entirely practical for one that already exists.

As an example, a theatre in London's West End – the London Coliseum – had a considerable number of disabled people on its patrons' circulation list. Yet the theatre itself was notoriously difficult to get to, with absolutely no on-street car parking close by, with wheelchair-user access restricted to the stalls only, and with only one accessible WC located in the queuing corridor for the ladies toilets. On first investigation with the newly formed access group, it quickly became clear that the support provided by the theatre staff was so much appreciated – pre-recorded scene descriptions for blind people, induction loops for deaf people and an intermission drinks service for those with mobility impairments – that these far outweighed the building's many limitations. For the group to therefore meet regularly at the theatre to discuss potential improvements with the project

Access consultation groups made up from people with different disabilities, all with a common interest in a particular historic building, can provide valuable insights into how things might be improved.

British Museum - level 02

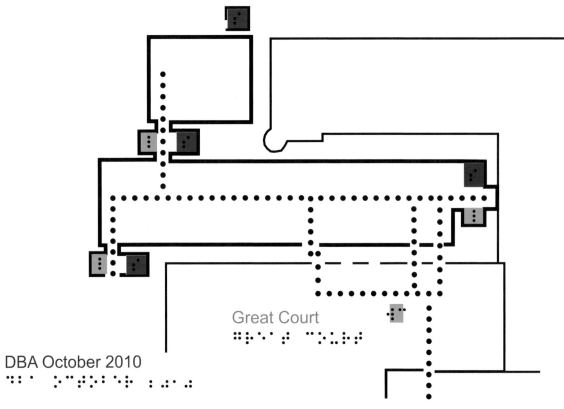

Great Court

DBA October 2010

This is a detail of a tactile plan produced for blind and partially sighted group members to understand the architect's proposals. In this case it concerns proposals for the location of a new lift in the British Museum.

design team was an instructive and enjoyable experience for everyone.

Each group member described their theatre visit experience based on their particular needs, allowing each to focus on what were often separate aspects of the project's ambitions. For example, wheelchair users and those unable to use stairs had much to say about the building's physical limitations; deaf and people with hearing impairment had much to say about equipment, and blind and partially sighted people about pre-performance information. For the project manager, each of these is likely to be addressed by separate budgets and consultants.

An alternative, but entirely compatible approach would be to follow the access guidelines published by

ACE and the HLF. Indeed, it was essential to complete these checklists for an application to be approved at each design stage. The lists are comprehensive and include a review of back-of-house provisions, such as changing rooms, stage access and, of course, the Green Room. Even if these areas are unfamiliar to group members, they should be well understood in principle by the supporting access consultant.

The overall purpose here is to allow periodic reviews of all these areas that are quite outside the scope of building regulations. The architect, theatre designers, exhibition designers and so on, will all be expected to present their proposals at a suitable point in the project programme. While the group will usually have no powers to accept or reject a proposal,

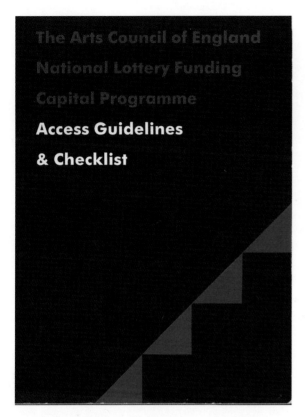

The Arts Council of England
National Lottery Funding
Capital Programme
**Access Guidelines
& Checklist**

The Arts Council of England's *Access Guidelines and Checklist* far exceeded the minimal requirements of the building regulations. It set a benchmark for standards in culture and arts buildings that still apply today. It was first published just after the Disability Discrimination Act 1995. This is the 1998 edition.

its views will go on record, having a potentially powerful influence on outcomes. In practice, the benefits of consulting an access group for upgrading and altering an historic building will vary, but the following benefits usually apply – visitor insights, careful interrogation of the design and continuity of the original project aims.

Insights – this is often the most revealing stage of the consultation process. It allows the team responsible for the building to understand and appreciate issues they might never otherwise have thought of. Preconceptions about the building's limitations can sometimes be debunked and unnecessary anxieties set aside. Of most importance, it allows priorities to be identified.

Interrogation – but this may seem a harsh term to describe a benefit, but it really is necessary to keep the initial access ambitions and commitments on the agenda. As a project proposal firms up, priorities will be challenged, as they always are, and some will be in danger of being forgotten. It will be for the group, often in partnership with the access consultant, to negotiate a way through the inevitable 'value engineering' process and ensure things stay on track.

Continuity – major projects can sometimes take several years to run from beginning to end. Memories can be short and members of the project team can come and go. An access group can provide valuable continuity and oversight, ensuring that the original aspirations and commitments are delivered.

Several of the case studies in this book benefitted from the input of an access group, notably Tate Britain, the Royal Festival Hall, the Roundhouse and Ironmonger Row Swimming Baths. It is perhaps no coincidence that these are among the most celebrated for their comprehensive accessibility.

Chapter Eleven

Looking Forward

Introduction

The usual advice is that to look forward we must first look back. That advice is followed in this chapter by first looking back at the early measures that brought accessibility and inclusive design onto the agenda of owners of historic buildings, the architects appointed to them and the disabled people who wished to use them. Almost all of these enabling measures have now ceased or are drawing to a close, not least where government funding was first provided but later withdrawn. Looking forward raises the question of what these recent developments mean for the future.

Given the changes put in place over the last fifty years, inclusive design is arguably now sufficiently a part of mainstream thinking that it cannot go into reverse. It has become part of the process of review now routinely undertaken by all public institutions and business corporations responsible for the delivery of services within an historic structure. In the UK the practical use of historic buildings, even when highly prized, continues to be the norm. The major upgrading of railway stations is an example, with their legacy of Victorian architecture skilfully adapted to new transportation standards.

Legislation

The preceding chapter makes clear the importance of a single piece of legislation, the Chronically Sick and Disabled Persons Act of 1970 enacted half a century ago. The Act made a direct connection between how buildings were designed and the life-chances of the disabled people who might need to use them.

OPPOSITE: The London Transport Museum in Covent Garden.

It took a quarter of a century for what, in 1970, was an encouragement to do something, to 1995 when action became a requirement backed up by law. The Disability Discrimination Act of 1995 set out a time-table for change, with 2005 as a deadline for physical barriers to accessibility to be addressed. The process of change had to be reported to parliament by a Disability Rights Commission and case law developed through the courts. Many of the prominent early activists involved still occupy positions of influence in government.

As the aims of the Disability Discrimination Act came about so, it was argued, the need for further specific disability legislation declined. Disability rights as an issue has in recent times become absorbed into the much broader spectrum of equal rights for all vulnerable groups, leading to the Equalities Act 2010. While this legislation will have some continued influence on building design, it is more directed towards policy and management. The likelihood of further disability-specific legislation for buildings must therefore be in doubt, but not least because its case has over recent years been successfully made.

Regulations

Running parallel with the development of legislation has been the introduction of access for disabled people into the national building regulations. The first tentative steps in 1985 only applied the regulations to new buildings, but a decade later they applied more widely to include older buildings, even those that were listed.

The first regulations made clear their limited application to the needs of people with mobility difficulties, principally wheelchair users. Addressing the access needs of wheelchair users and people unable to climb stairs continues to be a key issue for designers. All of the case studies in this book first set out with that objective in mind and this continues to be a benchmark of success. But the regulations have been updated several times since first published. This was in part to set out new requirements for blind and partially sighted people and for those who are deaf or hard of hearing. These additional considerations naturally extend to existing buildings as well as new, and often with little difficulty and at modest cost.

In the future it might be expected that the regulations will be yet further extended to consider aspects of building design that might help people with mental health and learning difficulties. If so, these are likely to refer to the benefits of effective signage and way-finding, both elements of design readily applied to historic buildings.

In conclusion, it is notable that the latest edition of regulations regarding access to buildings no longer refers to disabled people in the title. Instead, the need for accessibility is, by implication, deemed to apply to everyone.

The Role of Charities

The role of charities in providing for the 'sick and the poor' has played a long and significant part in English history that extends back well beyond the Poor Law Act of 1601. A key feature was localism, whereby buildings for the sick and poor were always close by. This was a necessity given the absence of transport other than walking or riding a horse, and funding was obtained from the local parish rather than from central government. In the nineteenth century, the new railways and canal systems caused a complete reversal of this arrangement, allowing new specialist institutions to be constructed away from the cities to rural locations. The county asylums are a notable example. The new rail and canal links allowed the rapid transportation of building materials and contractors, as well as the asylum residents, a pattern quickly followed by charitable institutions, such as those providing for disabled children. Chailey Heritage Craft School in Sussex, designed by father and son architects Ninian and Sebastian Comper, is just one example and Treloar College in Hampshire another. Located in the countryside, these special schools provided fresh air locations for city children with tuberculosis and were reached by the new rail links, with Treloars even having its own small railway station.

This arrangement of rural locations for asylums and special schools remained in place well into the twentieth century, suiting both the charities who ran them and the newly created county authorities that

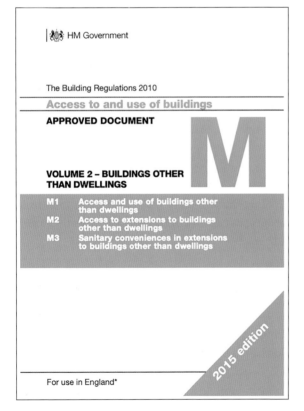

This is the latest edition of *Approved Document M* of the building regulations. Note that the term 'Disabled' has been omitted from the title, unlike the earlier versions that were entitled, *Access and facilities for Disabled People*.

St George's at Chailey Heritage in Sussex was designed by Ninian and Sebastian Comper just before the First World War. It was exclusively for disabled children but made no concessions for accessibility other than the installation of one lift. (Image provided by Chailey Heritage Foundation, www.chf.org.uk)

by now had a duty of care and who funded them. The attraction was, in part, the avoidance of any need to alter their many local schools and other educational buildings by making them accessible. Many specialist educational institutions for deaf people and blind people came into being in the first half of the twentieth century, with St Dunstan's in Brighton a rare modernist example. The increasing number of these schools further reduced any need for local schools and places of training to change.

By contrast, St Dunstan's College for the Blind was designed by Burnet Tait and Lorne in 1939. It included a multitude of special features with the specific purpose of enabling blind students to make best use of the building. (Photo: Architectural Press Archive/RIBA Collections)

In the 1970s this changed once more with the Warnock Report proposing community care in preference to care in remote rural institutions. Following the Education Act of 1983, the old charitable institutions dwindled in numbers as the new responsibility for community care was substantially placed on existing local organizations, a change that is still underway and will, in all likelihood, continue.

The implications of this important shift from special needs institutions to local provision are set out in Chapter 2, pointing out how many of the UK's historic buildings have had to adapt. This has been described as a 'silent revolution' in architecture, relentlessly moving forward and impacting on all the building case studies in the preceding chapters. For this process of change to now stop or go into reverse is almost inconceivable.

Disability Networks

The history of how disabled people themselves established local and national networks to press their demands on the relevant institutions to act is notable. The government helped create bodies such as the Access Committee for England and CAE, precisely for this purpose. Training was made available to enable disabled people to read plans and provide constructive criticism through newly created access consultation groups. By the 1990s there was in place a national network of two or three hundred such groups providing a strong influence on local authorities through representation on planning and other committees. They also provided a pool of skilled disabled participants able to join access consultation groups, as encouraged by the Arts Council and the HLF.

Following the withdrawal of government funding, most of these groups have now gone, inhibiting future scope for user consultation. Only in our major cities do they continue to do their work. This is arguably a real loss, especially to the historic buildings industry, where consultation groups offered so much

Access by Design was the journal of the Centre for Accessible Environments. At the time, the architect Louis Hellman produced cartoons for the front cover. Here is a classic 2004 Hellman cartoon charting the progress of inclusive design over the preceding three decades.

useful insight and encouragement to go that one step further. It would require a major programme of training to reverse this situation and while that may be unlikely, such a group was brought into being for the 2012 Olympic project in London and was sufficiently valued for it still to advise on new building developments in east London.

Looking forward, there could be a strong case for the National Trust as probably the largest single owner of our historic buildings to foster such a local network of access groups once more. Given the Trust's increasing reliance on the older population for their continued business, such collaboration could be of benefit to both parties.

The Business Case

The last fifty years have seen a complete change around from substantial reliance on specialist buildings designed for people with 'special needs', to an increased reliance on mainstream resources, including adapted existing buildings. As expectations have increased so too has the willingness to change, including a broad acceptance of these changes by the institutions responsible for building conservation.

This is not to say that disability legislation and regulations have significantly increased in recent years, they have not. Nor that pressure from disability groups has increased either, it has not and, if anything, has declined. But what has happened is an acceptance by the buildings industry that mainstream provision is in the wider interest of society and with some exceptions, makes for better business.

Apart from any sense of moral duty, what is referred to as 'the business case' has been a powerful incentive. This is the argument that the long-term survival of many historic buildings lies in part with their ability to provide continued and relevant use. This may be by increasing visitor numbers or attracting more funding by improving accessibility. The changing demographics of the UK and much of the world is towards an increasingly older population. This expanding group is well known as having both the time and inclination to visit our older buildings and while there, to spend money on buying tickets, enjoying refreshments, and purchasing books and gifts in the shops. This source of income is referred to as the 'grey pound', and can be expected to continue to help fund improvements to accessibility for years to come.

This argument is now well understood by both building owners and their architects and it draws attention to yet another future trend, the increasing competency and ingenuity of the profession. The case studies in the preceding chapters fully support this assertion. Compare, for example, the town hall ramp project of 1992 in Islington with that at Tate Britain just a few years later. The former provided step-free access into the building but with little other adaptation beyond the installation of an internal platform lift powered by an air compressor. A decade later in 2012, access at Tate Britain was comprehensively addressed throughout the entire building including a new entrance ramp, a new lift, accessible WCs and step-free access to all public spaces. Without doubt funding played its part, but improved architectural confidence played an important part also.

Professional Skills

Over recent years the architectural profession and its counterpart town planners and building surveyors have each developed new expertise on access to buildings in order to meet the demands of their clients and the funding agencies they often rely on. In addition a new kind of professional, the access consultant, has emerged to guide and advise on the subject. Professional credentials can now be relied on from the National Register of Access Consultants (NRAC), set up shortly after the Disability Discrimination Act 1995 and also the Access Association, a professional body promoting best practice.

The lottery institutions have been especially relevant to these developments, insisting on accessibility as a condition of funding. This has been such a successful incentive in the UK that it is probably fair to say that the subject is now sufficiently well embedded into the thinking and practice of the design professions that it is unlikely to go into reverse.

Similarly, the interest and encouragement of CABE have played a key role. This body was also funded initially by government and it published informative publications on the subject, helping define what inclusive design might mean. Following withdrawal of funding, CABE has been subsumed into the Design Council but its interest in promoting inclusive design continues as part of a wider argument for social sustainability.

These are the logos of some institutions that currently promote and maintain standards of accessibility as they apply to old and new buildings.

Continuing Professional Development (CPD) sessions on inclusive design, like those run by RIBA, continue to be a popular topic for architects in practice, though it still remains for the next generation of architects to be properly introduced to the subject at our schools of architecture.

Looking back over the last twenty-five years, what is striking but hardly surprising is the increase in confidence and ingenuity when conceiving access improvements to historic buildings. This has been in response in part to raised client expectations. Any major expenditure on an historic building in the UK will now, as a matter of course, address access issues, especially if public funding is to be relied on.

The architectural profession broadly understands this and has become more proficient, bolder even, in devising options. But mention must also be made of those bodies responsible for conservation that will have been encouraged by the quality of improvements in recent times. This is in contrast to twenty-five years ago when many proposals could be disappointing or at their worst, a source of dismay because of poor design. One by one these older schemes are themselves now the focus of change. We might be confident that this increase in competence and expertise will continue.

Mainstream Product Design

It is usually the case that the design and appearance of specialist equipment benefits considerably from exposure to mainstream demands. Power-operated doors, for example, once a special feature of hospitals and care homes, are now installed in most modern public buildings with expectations of reliability and a smart appearance. The sometimes novel but often ugly disability products of years ago have now mercifully disappeared. The same can be seen with the design of wheelchairs that for many years were standard products, over-engineered to their credit but heavy and difficult to use. Wheelchair development now aligns more with the bicycle industry, with vastly improved technology, lightweight materials and a range of choice, rather than with bulk hospital supplies. This is all relevant to historic buildings in that the range and appearance of products has improved sufficiently to gain the interest of architects.

Manufacturers of 'access' equipment, from handrails to lifts and ramps to stair nosings, have generally improved the appearance and design of their products. Discretion and style are prevailing over the earlier insistence on declaring a product as being 'for the disabled' through the unnecessary use of

Above is a very early version of a mechanical platform lift powered by an air compressor and bellows. It probably worked reasonably well but was not an item of beauty. By contrast, below is a platform lift installed in the Treasury and shows how product design has improved in just a few years.

bright colours and over-engineering. This change has been driven in part by the hotel industry now insistent on design and finish as well as on function. Platform lifts are a case in point where a highly sophisticated appearance is now possible rather than the off-the-shelf products of the past. These developments have some way yet to go but generally the direction is towards improved product appearance

more appropriate to the quality that an historic building conservation project deserves.

New Technology

A less explored area of 'change' is virtual or augmented reality. Virtual tours of major museums around the world already exist though their development is still in its infancy. They are no substitute for the real experience of a visit to these places, but virtual tours are, however, instantly available at any time, booking is not required and crowds and queuing are irrelevant. So too are the practicalities of travel or meticulous planning that can be essential for someone with limited mobility. The lockdown required to address the 2020 pandemic introduced a huge audience to virtual tours and experiences. It may be that this proves to be one of the 'silver linings' to emerge from the crisis.

Virtual tours could become an attractive idea if they were able to offer an alternative to actually visiting a building or even allowing less accessible areas and spaces to be more widely seen. It will continue to be inevitable that some exceptional rooms or spaces in historic buildings will remain inaccessible due to practical difficulties of access and overriding concerns for conservation. An example is the Octagon 'telescope' Room in Flamsteed House Royal Observatory at Greenwich. To install a lift for access would be inconceivable. However, what a wonderful experience it would be for a visitor unable to gain physical access to instead 'see' a virtual equivalent of the room and perhaps even enjoy a brief conversation there with a virtual Sir Christopher Wren.

The use of drones for aerial surveys and house viewings is no longer unusual and this technology is well suited to viewing historic buildings and their grounds in a wholly new way. A typical application might be Framlingham Castle in Suffolk where the fortified ramparts are of special interest and the

This early view of the Octagon Room at the Royal Observatory Greenwich has changed little over time. To introduce some form of lift for step-free access into this space would be difficult if not impossible to achieve. However, producing a virtual tour is highly possible and would allow enjoyment of this space even for those unable to visit.

The ramparts of Framlingham Castle can be reached by stairs from within this building, but to complete a circuit of the ramparts requires considerable agility. An aerial film using drone technology would bring this experience to a wide audience, especially people with limited mobility. (Photo: Dave Briggs, CC BY-SA 2.0, via Wikimedia Commons)

views from them quite exceptional, but to be enjoyed involves a difficult climb by stairs. A virtual tour or an aerial tour film using a drone are both now a practical and affordable option.

Looking forward, it is reasonable to assume and expect continued benefits from these types of new technologies, if nothing else than to 'show' a potential visitor with limited mobility how a visit to an historic building might be possible.

Summary

In summary, the business of improved accessibility has moved away from 'special needs' and more to 'mainstream' expectations. This better serves a growing cohort of disabled people, expanding in line with an increasingly older population. It also better serves those concerned with maintaining the integrity of our many historic buildings open to visitors.

Arts Council England (1994). *Guidance Notes on Access for Disabled People to Arts Venues.* Arts Council England.

Arts Council England (1998). *National Lottery Funding – Capital Programme – Access Guidelines and Checklist.*

Arts Council England. Cabinet Office (1994). *The Citizen's Charter and People with Disabilities – A Checklist.* HMSO.

Cave, A. (2007). *Museums and Art Galleries – Making Buildings Accessible.* RIBA Publishing.

Commission for Architecture and the Built Environment (2004). Commission for Architecture and the Built Environment (2006). Department of Communities and Local Government (2015). Approved Document Part M. Vol. 2. *Access to Buildings Other than Dwellings.* Department of Communities and Local Government.

Department for Transport's Code of Practice Accessible Train Station Design For Disabled People (2011).

Design Standards for Accessible Railway Stations. Version 04 2015. Department of Transport. (2011).

Cave, A. (2007). *Museums and Art Galleries – making Buildings Accessible.* RIBA Publishing.

Building Regulations: Approved Document Part M (2015). *Volume 2 – Access to Buildings other than Dwellings.* Department of Communities and Local Government.

Earnscliffe, J. (2019). *Building Access: A good Practice Guide for Arts and Culture Organisations.* Arts Council England.

English Heritage (1995). English Heritage (2015). *Easy Access to Historic Buildings.* English Heritage Publishing.

English Heritage (2015). *Easy Access to Historic Landscape.* English Heritage Publishing.

Fleck, J. (2019). *Are you an Inclusive Designer?* RIBA Publishing.

Historic England. (2018). *Streets for All: Advice for Highways and Public Realm Works in Historic Places.* English Heritage Publishing .

Holmes-siedle, J. (1996). *Barrier-free Design: A Manual for Building Designers and Managers.* Routledge Publishing.

Massie, Sir B. (2019). *A Life without Limits.* Merio Books.

Ministry of Housing, Communities and Local Government (2019). *National Planning Policy Framework.* Ministry of Housing, Communities and Local Government.

Museums and Galleries Commission (1995). *Guidelines on Disability for Museums and Galleries in the United Kingdom.* Museums and Galleries Commission.

RELATED TITLES FROM CROWOOD

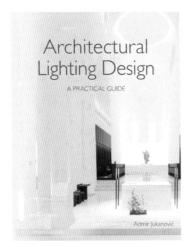

978 1 78500 457 5

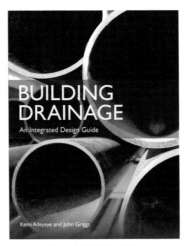

978 1 78500 639 5

978 1 78500 870 2

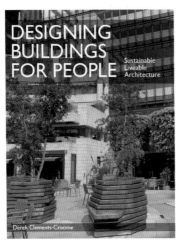

9 781 78500 709 5

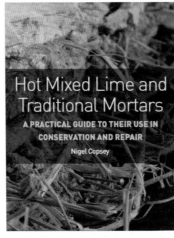

978 1 78500 555 8

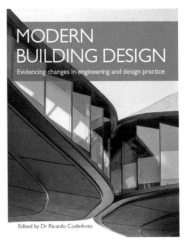

9 781 78500 663 0

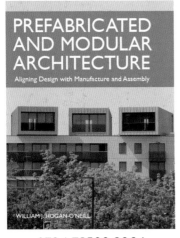

978 1 78500 806 1

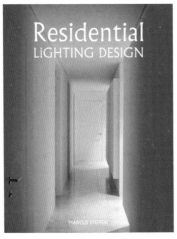

978 1 84797 756 4

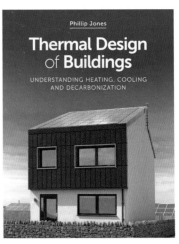

978 1 78500 898 6